EARLY CHILDHOOD EDUCATION SERIES

Leslie R. Williams, Editor

Millie Almy, Senior Advisor

ADVISORY BOARD: **Barbara T. Bowman, Harriet K. Cuffaro, Stephanie Feeney, Doris Pronin Fromberg, Celia Genishi, Stacie G. Goffin, Dominic F. Gullo, Alice Sterling Honig, Elizabeth Jones, Gwen Morgan, David Weikert**

(Continued)

Experimenting with the World

John Dewey and the
Early Childhood Classroom

Harriet K. Cuffaro

Teachers College, Columbia University
New York and London

Published by Teachers College Press, 1234 Amsterdam Avenue
New York, NY 10027

Library of Congress Cataloging-in-Publication Data

Cuffaro, Harriet K.
    Experimenting with the world : John Dewey and the early childhood
classroom / Harriet K. Cuffaro.
        p.   cm. – (Early childhood education series)
    Includes bibliographical references and index.
    ISBN 0-8077-3372-5 (acid-free paper). – ISBN 0-8077-3371-1 (pbk.
: acid-free ppaper)
    1. Early childhood education. 2. Dewey, John, 1859–1952.
3. Dewey, John, 1859–1952–Bibliography. I. Title. II. Series.
LB1139.23.C84 1995
372.21–dc20   94-25503

ISBN 0-8077-3372-5
ISBN 0-8077-3371-7 (pbk.)

Printed on acid-free paper

Manufactured in the United States of America

98 97 96 95   8 7 6 5 4 3 2 1

For
Angelo and Nina
Kalligeris

εὐχαριστῶ

Contents

Acknowledgments

No book is written alone. It is encouraged, critiqued, questioned, and supported by the presence of the people to whom we turn in the struggle of writing and the thinking through of ideas. This is my opportunity to express my thanks for the countless conversations, the illuminating questions, the gentle and not so gentle prodding to "get on with it," and the encouragement that helped greatly to bring this project to completion.

What I have gained from the spirit, the culture, and the people in two educational communities is an intrinsic part of this book. At the City and Country School founded by Caroline Pratt and at the Bank Street College of Education I have had the opportunity to share and live ideals and to experience the meaning of associated living. For all our conversations, questions, disagreements, and discussions I am deeply grateful. Our talk and stories challenged me to search for fundamental beliefs within changing contexts.

Most recently, my work and research with early childhood educators in Iceland have added immeasurably to my understanding of teachers' thinking, and my own thinking about the influence of culture on the aesthetics of teaching and learning. To my colleagues in Reykjavik, a heartfelt *tak*.

I would like to thank Leslie R. Williams for her generous support and Joseph C. Grannis for his probing comments as I began my journey into Dewey. I wish to express my gratitude to Judith Chiti, Ellen Condliffe Lagemann, Miriam Raider-Roth, Edna Shapiro, and Jonathan G. Silin for their sensitive reading, thought-provoking comments, and clarifying questions—and for the laughter and friendship that sustain—as the end came into view and this book and journey neared completion.

At Teachers College Press my thanks to Carole Saltz and Sarah Biondello for their support, and particularly to Susan Liddicoat, who with great patience shared the complexities that surfaced as I searched to find a citation style that lent itself to conversations.

To my husband Gastone, both for his support and encouragement and for the impatience that prodded me to finish, and for accepting John Dewey as a member of our family—my very special thanks.

This book is dedicated to my parents, who honored with honesty the "whys" I asked and who supported my searching.

A Note on Citations and Readings

Wishing to acknowledge the extraordinary accomplishment and scholarship represented in the publication of *The Collected Works of John Dewey* by Southern Illinois University Press, I have provided a double citation for all Dewey quotes. In the form I have used, the reader is referred first to commonly found editions of individual books by Dewey. The second citation refers to *The Collected Works* published by Southern Illinois University Press edited by Jo Ann Boydston. The 34 volumes of *The Collected Works* are divided into three parts—The Early Works 1882–1898, The Middle Works 1899–1924, The Later Works 1925–1953. To illustrate what the reader will find, the source of a quote from *Democracy and Education* appears as (DE, 32; MW 9:41). DE stands for the title of the work and is followed by the page number. After the semicolon, MW 9 refers to the Middle Works, Volume 9, and is followed by a colon and the page number. The bibliography contains full citations plus the key to the abbreviations used for book and essay titles.

In addition to the writings by Dewey, included in the bibliography are writings about Dewey and other books that have informed my thinking. At the end of each chapter related readings are included.

I wish to express my appreciation to Southern Illinois University Press for permission to quote extensively from *The Collected Works*, and in particular to Gipsey Hicks of the Press who guided me through the process.

Experimenting with the World

John Dewey and the
Early Childhood Classroom

1

A Teacher's Perspective

Philosophy is thinking what the known demands of us, what responsive attitude it exacts. It is an idea of what is possible, not a record of accomplished fact. Hence it is hypothetical like all thinking. It presents an assignment of something to be done – something to be tried. Its value lies not in furnishing solutions (which can be achieved only in action) but in defining difficulties and suggesting methods for dealing with them. Philosophy might also be described as thinking which has become conscious of itself – which has generalized its place, function, and value in experience.

(DE, 326; MW 9:336)

A basic assumption of this book is my belief that it is essential in teaching that practice be grounded in a consciously held, critically examined philosophical framework created by the teacher. A philosophy of education represents the choices, values, knowledge, and beliefs of teachers as well as their aspirations, intentions, and aims. It serves to guide and inspire and contributes to determining the detail of the everyday life in the classroom. The broad, general theme of the importance and determining influence of a philosophy of education is particularized and illustrated in this book by examining and articulating how a particular educational philosophy, that of John Dewey, informs practice and speaks to the detail of classroom life. A tension exists in dealing with the two themes, the importance of a philosophical framework and the examination of Dewey's thought: to avoid the implication that Dewey's philosophy is *the* framework or philosophy to guide practice. This is not a guide to "doing Dewey." What is offered is an unfolding and connecting of Dewey's educational philosophy from a teacher's perspective, how his thought may be understood while situated in the complexities and activities of daily

1

classroom life. My focus on the importance of a philosophical framework is rooted in my biography, in the culture of my home, and the way my family viewed and approached life.

THE PERSONAL *I*

As a first generation Greek-American I grew up with stories that were set in far away locations, places I had never seen. I was told stories of experiences that were dramatically compelling and also distant from my present. The stories I heard, of past and present, were stories of the immigrant experience, which repeatedly connected cause and effect and were filled with detailed explanations that included the *why* of each story.

I learned of life in the Greek community of Turkey, of eventual displacement and refugee living following the burning of Smyrna, times of separation and disorientation, and comic episodes that lightened loneliness. Listening to their stories, I traveled with them till they settled in Egypt in another Greek community in Alexandria, and then once again followed the move of family and friends, one after another, to New York City. Everyone had a story to tell and through their repeated stories the far away became as familiar and known as the streets on which I played in New York City. My hyphenated identity of Greek-American was a construct of others, because I lived in a world where the "explainers" of the why of living spoke from a framework that preserved a primarily Greek identity. And, as I was often told, it was an identity that had been maintained during "five hundred years of oppression and must not be lost now in one generation." Identity carried with it family and national history as well as moral obligation.

While protected, the culture in which I lived was also permeable. It had been and was influenced in different ways by the majority cultures in which it had existed—Turkey, Egypt, America—and also by the fact that my father had been a seaman for 15 years, an odyssey that began in his mid-teens. The stories of his years on the sea made the world a personal and human place. Geography, economics, history, anthropology, and politics became real through the stories of people's lives in China, India, the ports of Africa and South America, and successful passages through the Suez and Panama canals. Again the world was explained through stories of people and their experiences, their lives in a world that offered both opportunities and disappointments, beginnings and endings, constancy and diversity. The stories of my family primed me to attend to the social, to community, and to the political context of people's experiences. The culture of my home laid the foundation for my search, and need, for a philosophy of education when I became a teacher. And from this mix of rules and dreams, of laughter and responsibility, of past and present connected, I constructed the beliefs and values with which I came to teaching.

THE PUBLIC *WE*

My first full-time teaching position was with the four-year-old group at the City and Country School founded by Caroline Pratt. I began in September with a wealth of information about transitions, rest, lunch, many songs, and openness to blocks and children's play. The teacher education program I had completed sensitized me to a "whole child" perspective, which attended to the social, emotional, intellectual, and physical needs of the child. Knowledge of child development was in the forefront of my thinking. It was in that first year of teaching at the school, in conversations with other teachers and at our staff meetings, that I began to realize that the development of curriculum was more than what one learned in courses.

What caused upheaval of the conglomeration of child development, learned techniques, "musts" of early childhood curriculum, and the personal values that together constituted the framework from which I functioned, was the way the City and Country teachers thought about materials and children's experiences. They questioned what I took for granted and saw what I had not thought about or imagined. It was clear that there was a City and Country way of thinking and acting. The philosophy of the school had detail, coherence, and the obvious commitment of the teachers. I worked hard at teasing out the detail for myself, making connections, and matching my emerging view of teaching with what I saw and heard daily. Influenced by the experience of working a year with the same group of children and the conversations with the other teachers in the school, I was experiencing a shift in my thinking. While child development was still an essential factor in my planning, I thought less in terms of stages and characteristics. Constructs about children began to give way to named children who were alive and present in the room and I began to give more attention to what I wanted them to learn.

The personal values and beliefs with which I came to teaching had been explicitly stated. I was born into them, surrounded by them, and frequently reminded of them. City and Country reasons for doing and being—the school's values, language, and culture—I had to search for and translate. One source of enlightenment was Caroline Pratt's *I Learn From Children* (1948). Another was the teachers who had worked in the school for many years. A bit unsettling to my need for certainty, and approval, was the variety I found in interpretations. And there were also the times when a child would surprise me and make me pause, as Judie did. One morning while I was planting seeds with a small group of children and being quite directive (although I saw my behavior as open to the children's interests and participation), Judie suddenly thrust her plant at me and said vehemently, "Here's *your* plant! I don't want it." I then had to face the discrepancy between my stated aims and my actual behavior, the distance between my limiting openness and the openness to which I aspired. All the thinking and rethinking, the questioning and self-evaluation, made me feel vulnerable because teaching is so public.

Central to all my thinking was coming to understand how a school created a sense of community. At City and Country, community was an all-permeating priority. *We* was used frequently. *We* was a reason, not only an identifying label. It was not an empty word or form. It was a constant reminder of one's connectedness with others. I came to teaching valuing community. I had grown up surrounded by it. Now I had to think about how I would create and maintain community in a classroom of diverse four-year-olds striving to declare their individuality and independence.

I have lingered in describing aspects of my experience at City and Country because the years I worked in the school had a profound influence on how I view teaching and the teacher I am. Beginning in a school with a clearly articulated and lived philosophy, a philosophy in which community was central, gave me familiar support while I worked to create my teaching self.

Later, teaching primary grades in a public school system introduced me to curriculum guides and working within a large bureaucratic system. Here there was not an articulated philosophy with which to contend, but regulations, rules that were seldom open to discussion. In these years I learned how to shape and bend the given—curriculum guides with their chosen content—to the interests and skills of the children; how to search out openings for activity in work patterns that were predominantly sedentary; and how to free time and space from a segmented schedule for the children and myself. These were among the more difficult challenges I faced as a teacher.

At another time, working as a kindergarten teacher at a therapeutic preschool in a research setting enriched my understanding of the multiple meanings of children's behavior. The psychoanalytic perspective of the school introduced yet another framework to consider. As a teacher in a team of social workers, psychologists, and psychiatrists, I participated in discussions that helped me to clarify the domain of teaching as it contrasted with the work of therapist and family worker. My understanding of the function and significance of play was rotated and refined as play was discussed in the context of classroom and therapy sessions. In this setting the present–future–reality orientation of teaching was sharpened and the writing of daily observations, the recording of classroom life, became a part of and essential to teaching.

In highlighting some of my experiences as a classroom teacher, I may appear to be describing a journey of questioning and trying that is linear, with one step leading to another, a progression of growth. That was not how it happened nor did it occur in the order presented. There were times of tiredness and frustration when, consciously or unconsciously, I turned away from challenge, and times of immediacy when I acted in ways I found difficult to accept and struggled to understand. As a beginning teacher my world had been immediate. It was my classroom. I did not think in terms of a philosophy of education, although the phrase had been mentioned in college classes. What I had learned in classes and experienced in student teaching was that to which I turned but it was not really mine. It belonged to the teachers I selectively imitated, became, emulated. What I needed was time in my own classroom to select and discard, time to try and make sense, time to create *my* teaching self, time to achieve my integrity.

Over the years of working with children of different ages and their families in varied settings, I gradually created a firm foundation for teaching, which also included continuing questions and unknowns. From experience, I had developed that extra teaching sense, the ever present alertness to the social atmosphere that responds to unspoken cues and to the flow and sound of activity. Conversations with other teachers and directors, the discussions with student teachers about the what and why of children's behavior and curriculum development, and the meetings and talk with parents – all were means for thinking about and explaining to myself the connections I sought and made in relation to teaching. Talking with parents, describing and explaining how all the hours spent in painting, discussions, and building, in experimenting with water or clay, were important steps in learning to read and write; or explaining to a principal that the hour taken from the math program in order to take a trip did not mean lost math time, math was still there, although unscheduled, in the questions and activities generated by the trip – all were situations in which I gave form to and strengthened the connections between theory and practice. Connecting the lived experiences of the classroom with what I hoped for, valued, and chose became easier, although not less complex. The framework for teaching that I had created was tested when I left classroom teaching to join the faculty at Bank Street College of Education, yet another setting with an articulated philosophy that, like City and Country's, was rooted in the ideas and aspirations of progressive education.

The move from teaching children to adults, from standing in the midst of active children to sitting in an office, from acting in my own classroom to observing the actions of teachers in their classrooms (and having lunch without thinking about transitions, spilled milk, or lunch duty) was a new and sometimes unsettling way of being a teacher. When I visited the classrooms of the teachers I supervised, we talked about individual children, "the group," and schedules. We planned social studies and science activities. We moved furniture to create better traffic patterns and "smoothed" transitions. We thought about and discussed the surface and organizing content of curriculum (Bussis, Chittenden, & Amarel, 1976). We sought to connect what one observes in the materials and activities of a classroom, the surface level of teaching, with the deeper level of teaching that consists of teachers' aims, their priorities, and their knowledge of children, materials, and activities. Connecting the visible with the invisible of teaching, meant connecting the *what* of curriculum with the *what for* of curriculum. It was in varied settings, both public and private, with groups ranging from toddlers to third and fourth graders, that the framework I had created encountered other realities and possibilities, and conditions that were not supportive of growth. Often difficult for me to understand was that many of the settings, from established institutions to storefronts, offered the teachers with whom I worked little or no framework or direction to guide practice. As I shared with the teachers their personal questions and dilemmas, I also searched within myself. Beyond health and safety standards, were there *givens* that applied to early childhood settings from toddlers to primary grades? Whose givens? And, in what did my authority rest? In our work together, I tried to connect the *how, what, where,* and *when* questions, echoes of my own questioning, to the more fundamental question: *why?* While I shared my whys, what I hoped would grow out of our work together was that the teachers would consciously create their own framework, would piece together their understandings, knowledge, aims, and values into a functioning whole, where thinking would "become conscious of itself," where thinking and acting would join to become an idea of what is possible.

Developing a coherent whole, becoming philosophical about teaching, was not the agenda of every teacher with whom I worked, and that gave me pause. I tried to find new ways to provoke reflection and searched for catalysts that would surface questioning. I hoped that the questions I offered would in time lead to making deeper connections. Questions possess the power to surface even when not attended to; they linger. With other teachers, questioning became a way of relating, often with humor, and led to conversations that started with, "So, I asked myself 'why do I want to do this' because *I knew* that sooner or later you'd find a way to ask me." This was not like the incident with Judie and the flower pot because from the beginning of our work together, conversation and questioning were established as ways of learning, and it was understood that each of us would have questions to ask. For me, the experience of participant observer provided the distance that caused me to revisit and reflect on my own established meanings and in retrospect, I believe, pushed me to seek a larger, broader context into which each of us could place our particular, personal meanings and the experience of teaching.

ENCOUNTERING DEWEY

In my last year of classroom teaching, while writing my master's thesis, I read John Dewey's *Experience and Education* (1938; LW 13). It was an extraordinary experience. In an astonishing and curious way the book unified all my years of classroom teaching. Parts came together. I seemed to find the "ands," "ifs," and "buts" that completed thoughts I had left unfinished. What Dewey offered was familiar; his words certainly resonated with my experiences at City and Country. What I found in this first reading of Dewey was not answers but a way of thinking about teaching that enlarged purpose. Looking back, I wonder if, as I prepared to leave the classroom, I had started to look beyond my classroom with a new perspective.

I can turn to a Deweyan vocabulary and say that reading *Experience and Education* was a "moving experience" both in that it served as a catalyst and also in that it touched me deeply. In my first reading I underlined certain passages that spoke directly to me. Subsequent readings led to further underlining and exclamations of "How did I miss *that*?" I have wondered what I would learn about myself if I had used different colors to underline passages each time I read the book. Would I have found the story of the connections I made and the experiences that shaped my thinking? *Experience and Education* became a book to which I turned for the thought it contained, and with time it became like a map leading to further readings in Dewey. For example, in *Experience and Education* there is a sentence, "Everything depends upon the *quality* of the experience which is had" (EE, 27; LW 13:13). I read that sentence many times in my rereadings of the book and accepted it at face value – quality is quality – until the time I paused and asked, "What does *he* mean by quality?" "What *is* quality?" That began a search in Dewey's writings and in secondary sources and so my understanding expanded. Gradually a whole began to emerge as I made more connections.

That process was repeated many times until it became a way of reading Dewey and thinking about his ideas as questions surfaced in the dilemmas of teaching. As my reading of Dewey expanded I discovered that an idea presented in one sentence in a book became several paragraphs in another, and those paragraphs, in yet another book, became a chapter or an essay. My understanding of Dewey was deepened further, and also shaken, when I assigned *Experience and Education* in the curriculum course I began to teach at Bank Street College. I asked students to write a paper examining the ideas Dewey presented and to connect them to their own experiences as student or teacher. There were students who genuinely enriched my understanding of Dewey through their original and perceptive thinking, who probed deeply within themselves to connect past experiences with their newfound teaching self. There were students who directed me to gaps in my understanding as they made their connections, which caused me to rethink my own. And there were students who found Dewey lacking because he did not address their issues, which led me to search in other Dewey writings for the presence or absence of their interests.

The questions of students in courses, questions from teachers in their classrooms, and my own questions—all had a cumulative effect and set the foundation for a more formal study of Dewey's thought. What I discovered as I became more systematic in my reading of Dewey, and also turned to writings about Dewey, was the variety in interpreting his work. While my knowledge of Dewey was expanded and new dimensions were added to my thinking in seeing his work from the perspective of a philosopher or historian, this did not always lead to making or finding the connections I needed for the world of teaching. It would be misleading to assume from these comments that teachers are not interested in philosophy and history or that they lack depth in their thinking. Simply, it was that at the time of my reading we differed in what we chose to look at and question. Questions have their own time of importance; situations make them pertinent. To expand my own interpretation, I was searching for a view of Dewey as he would be understood while standing in a classroom in the midst of active children. Then, from that position how would Dewey's ideas be interpreted? It was in studying the work and writings of the "dauntless women" who were inspired by the educational and social ideas of progressivism—Caroline Pratt, Anna Bryan, Harriet Johnson, Lucy Sprague Mitchell, Patty Smith Hill, Alice Temple—complemented by the perspective of historians, philosophers, and others, that I achieved greater coherence in thinking about and using Dewey's philosophy of education in my work.

LOOKING AT TEACHERS AND TEACHING

Thinking about and dealing with two themes—the importance and determining influence of a philosophical framework and the unfolding and connecting of certain aspects of Dewey's educational philosophy—involves a delicate act of balancing. When the two themes are brought together, the latter serves to illustrate the meaning and intention of the former. Implicit in my thinking, interwoven in the two themes, is my view of the teacher as a decision maker—a view not shared in the research literature on teaching until the early 1980s. Now there is little question that teachers are seen as decision makers as the focus of research on teaching has shifted to examine the thinking of teachers in the multiple decisions they make daily (Clark & Peterson, 1986). Within the proliferating literature on teacher thinking, diverse perspectives and interests are evident, such as: how teachers manage the complexities of classroom teaching (Berlak & Berlak, 1981); teachers' perception of and response to dilemmas (Lampert, 1985); the personal, practical knowledge of teachers (Connelly & Clandinin, 1985, 1988; Elbaz, 1983); teachers in relation to curriculum, teachers as "curriculum makers" (Clandinin & Connelly, 1992). As the thinking of teachers has been viewed in increasing detail, a complementary literature on narrative, teacher stories, and teacher lore also has emerged (Ayers, 1989; Carter, 1993; Elbaz, 1991; Paley, 1979,1981; Schubert, 1991; Witherell & Noddings, 1991; Yonemura, 1986). In this literature teachers' thinking is revealed through their own storytelling or in partnership with the researcher.

From the perspective of a classroom teacher, an identity that remains paramount as most of my time continues to be in classrooms, the acknowledgment of the complexity of teacher thinking is long awaited and welcome. It evokes a sigh of relief. For too long teachers have been described as faceless constants, not unlike furniture found in the classroom, mechanically enacting and implementing the ideas and plans of others. What was too often neglected or understood in these portraits were the conditions and systems that implicitly and explicitly silenced teachers and thwarted the emergence of imaginative teaching. Many teacher education institutions contributed to the reality of these portrayals with programs that focused primarily on a how-to mentality, the acquisition of techniques, and the meeting of certification requirements.

The current literature presents teachers with a truly human face. Teachers are seen in their individuality, people with concerns, dilemmas, values, and beliefs, consciously present in their teaching. The complexities of the contexts in which they work are also more fully acknowledged: the priorities, competing interests, and politics of the systems in which they teach; the poverty, struggle, and hopelessness of families that are the experienced life of many of the children who come to school each day.

As we, teachers and researchers, find our way in this new relationship, as teachers' voices are now elicited, questions arise about power and control, language and perspective. Once again it is the researcher's portrait that is displayed publicly. The more empathic and respectful entrance into the world of teachers by researchers in recent years, at times, still retains remnants of past images and relationships. Speaking generally, the perspective of some researchers continues to separate thought from the actions of teachers. The continued use of the word *practitioner;* the focus on teachers' actions and practice that often minimizes the thought embedded in action; and interpretations of unarticulated, undefined practice that often accompany discussions of teachers' tacit knowledge—all contribute to fragmenting the whole that teachers create, the whole that is self-teaching. Closer to understanding the nuanced meanings of the experience of teaching are the perceptive distinctions Elbaz (1991) makes in her discussion of the varied perspectives and constructs of researchers, their implicit paradigms, and their ways of knowing that lead to different interpretations of teaching. Similarly, Lampert's (1985) image of the teacher as a "dilemma manager" with the capacity for "invention and improvisation" in coping with situations reflects the everydayness of teaching. Understanding that dilemmas are approached not as something to solve but as those moments that ask us to surface our considerations—to put into view the claims that shape our actions—and to make choices among competing demands is to be present in the reality of teaching. Dilemmas appear when the social atmosphere gives permission to students to express their individuality. Dilemmas also appear when one holds a consciously articulated framework of valued preferences that guide teaching. Whatever the source, dilemmas appear when the unexpected occurs to disrupt what has been planned and imagined. Teaching is filled with such moments because we are always interacting with others and within self.

While seeking to understand the thinking and concerns of teachers mainly through observations and extended conversations or interviews with individual teachers, sufficient attention has not been given to the conversations among teachers, teachers talking with each other about their work, what I and many other teachers call "teacher talk." These conversations, often unplanned, take place daily, sometimes as an outgrowth of our inner, unheard monologues as we respond to the activities in our classrooms. There are also instances in which these conversations among teachers are a planned part of their work, such as the networks teachers have created in various cities and some of the programs that grew out of the open classrooms of the 1970s and continue today. Another instance in which teacher talk is honored is in the activities and planning of the Institute for Democratic Education (Wood, 1988). In all these varied settings for teacher talk what is evident is the searching of teachers for coherence in their work, their desire to refine the connections between the *what* and *what for* of teaching so that teaching makes sense not only to those with whom they work but also to self.

SEARCHING FOR MEANING AND COHERENCE

In all the research about teacher thinking little is said about teachers being philosophical or guided by a philosophy of education. There is reference to a teacher's perspective or framework, words that might be seen as synonymous with a philosophy of education. But these words seem in some way to stop short of declaration, a declaration of the self who has constructed the framework, the person who sees from a particular perspective. As I grapple to articulate the distinctions I sense in thinking about these words, present is my wish to select the word that comes closest to both my view of teaching as well as what I want teaching to be. Possibly, I may be reaching for language used in the past by teachers—and also their passion—who in their talk about curriculum willingly declared their choices concerning what knowledge was worth knowing and their vision of society. Implicit within those discussions, that teacher talk, was a moral and political sense, a vision and purposefulness in doing that went beyond the walls of the classroom.

Present within any philosophy of education are certain basic elements: a view of the learner and teacher, and the choices that have been made about knowledge. Is the learner a blank slate? Intrinsically or extrinsically motivated? Is the teacher to transmit, guide, facilitate, direct, enact, initiate? Is the knowledge chosen fixed, changing, grade level skills, facts, information? Is knowledge revealed, found, constructed? As we respond to these questions, the choices we make reveal our view of human nature and declare what we deem important and valued. What we choose to think about while creating our philosophical framework, how we think about questions, which parts we select for consideration, what attention we give to myths and stereotypes, all combine to determine the quality of life in a classroom and the possibilities it will hold for children and adults.

What follows in the coming chapters is the detail of my unfolding and connecting of Dewey's thought from the map that began while I was reading *Experience and Education*. It is my map but what makes it more than my own is that it has been redrawn time and again in countless conversations with teachers. Our struggles to find our way in the classroom dilemmas we faced, our talk about children and curriculum, created points of orientation. Our recurring questions and concerns indicated paths to explore and common vantage points from which to survey the world of teaching. The two concepts from Dewey's thought that have been selected

for examination—*the social individual* and *experience*—have been chosen because together they speak to some of the fundamental concerns of teachers: our view of human nature and learning, and how we consider and
balance the interests and needs of the individual and the group.

Chapters 2, 3, and 4 are interconnected. Chapter 2 introduces the
person in Dewey—the social individual—and Dewey's vision of democracy.
Chapter 3 places the social individual in an early childhood setting and
poses questions related to the development of curriculum. To what
choices does Dewey's view of the person lead in thinking about space,
materials, and time? What environment will support and maintain the
sense of community and the communication essential to democracy?
Chapter 4 examines the partnership between children and teachers in developing curriculum and also brings to the forefront the moral sense that
permeates Dewey's educational philosophy. Also included in Chapter 4 is
an extended anecdote of dramatic play and it is used to bring together the
ideas presented in these interconnected chapters.

Chapters 5, 6, and 7 have the same rhythm. Now the center of
attention is Dewey's concept of experience. Chapter 5 examines experience
both in its variety and detail. As experience is what people do and have,
the discussion of experience reaches back and connects to the social individual of the previous chapters. Chapter 6 locates the concept of experience in an early childhood setting and explores the meaning of the phrase
"to learn from experience." Questions raised earlier about curriculum are
revisited, now with a focus on experience. With experience as the vantage
point, connections are made to play and materials. Chapter 7 is another
extended anecdote of dramatic play and is used to illustrate both the
variety in experience and learning from experience.

Chapter 8 returns to the personal and to the difficulties encountered
in connecting Dewey's thought and vision with the daily life of the classroom. The personal is enlarged as Dewey is viewed through the lens of
today's classrooms.

While what Dewey offers is, I believe, applicable to education at any
age level, I have concentrated on the years of early childhood, particularly
the midpoint of four- to six-year-olds. Also in the extended anecdotes of
Chapters 4 and 7, I have turned each time to dramatic play connected to
block building. I am aware that not every early childhood teacher gives
such a prominent place or attention to blocks in the curriculum and that
my use of blocks to illustrate ideas may not be useful to all readers. Yet, it
is in such dramatic play where children symbolically re-present their
worlds, set the agenda, and create the situations that elicit interaction, that
I have found the questions and concerns, the problems and resolutions,
and the continuity of children's imaginative "experiment with the world"

expressed most clearly and directly. Blocks and dramatic play may not be the primary choice of many teachers as means for learning and teaching. And, increasingly, there are many kindergarten and primary classrooms where there are few blocks to be found. In the absence of blocks what may be taken from the anecdotal material in which blocks are central is the spirit of play–the experimentation, activity, participation and imagination that play invites and in which the vital, dynamic presence of children's personal questions, interests, and searching is a welcome contribution.

One of the challenges in writing this book has been to find a way in which to talk about teaching, the determining influence and support of a philosophical framework, and John Dewey, so that it has meaning beyond my own personal story and searching. It was when I understood that the process of unfolding and connecting Dewey's thought was made up of conversations–between Dewey and myself and also with other teachers–that I found the voice I sought, the rhythm that is present in teacher talk. My voice includes the voices of the teachers with whom I have worked and the students in courses I have taught. Dewey's voice is heard in the quotes from his writings. The children are present consistently as the focus of our conversations–conversations that proceed without the presence of many other voices referring to other sources or citing comparisons to similar ideas. Related readings will be found at the end of chapters. The bibliography contains full citations for references and additional texts of interest.

RELATED READINGS

Altenbaugh, R. J. (Ed.). (1992). *The teacher's voice: A social history of teaching in twentieth century America*. London: Falmer Press.

Perrone, V. (1991). *A letter to teachers: Reflections on schooling and the art of teaching*. San Francisco: Jossey-Bass.

Pratt, C. (1948). *I learn from children*. New York: Simon & Schuster.

Van Manen, M. (1990). *Researching lived experiences: Human science for an action sensitive pedagogy*. Albany: State University of New York Press.

2

The Social Individual:
Achieving Self in Context

I believe that the psychological and social sides are organically related and that education cannot be regarded as a compromise between the two, or a superimposition of one upon the other.

(PC, 21; EW 5:85)

In sum, I believe that the individual who is to be educated is a social individual and that society is an organic union of individuals. If we eliminate the social factor from the child we are left with an abstraction; if we eliminate the individual factor from society, we are left only with an inert and lifeless mass.

(PC, 22; EW 5:86)

Early childhood teachers are storytellers. Each day we have at least two or three stories to share. With our anecdotes, as we describe children's accomplishments, their struggles, and their discoveries, we enrich our understanding of the children with whom we work. As we tell our stories, we carefully set the context ("We had just settled down for music . . . "). We introduce the characters ("and sitting next to Brian was Jenny who is BOSS of everything this week—and he has such difficulty asserting himself . . . "). We try to make sense and find connections ("What helped Brian speak up for himself today—especially to Jenny? Earlier in the day he came to tell me about his drawing. That was unusual for him . . . "). Our anecdotes are cumulative, not isolated incidents. With each vignette, with each situation we describe, we add further detail and nuance, yet another chapter in the story of each child.

With our anecdotes, we tell as much about ourselves, the storytellers, as we do about the children we describe. What surprises us, what is worth noting and telling, as well as how we fit pieces together to construct our narratives, reflects our experiences in and our view of the world. Shaping and coloring our stories and our aims are our values and beliefs. How we see, what we select, and what we find meaningful are rooted in our histories—the people we have known, the places we have passed and lived in, the stories and myths we have heard, the textures we have touched and tasted. Our personal preferences, both changing and stable over time, are ever present as we encounter the world and as we respond to children.

Without question, as teachers of young children our vision and our stories also are influenced by theories of development. Depending on the program of teacher education and which theorist had prominence at the time, children may be viewed through the lens of Vygotsky, Piaget, or Erikson or described in terms of a behavioral, psychoanalytic, maturationist, or constructivist perspective. The settings in which we work, and shifting societal concerns, also influence what we focus on and talk about— whether our anecdotes are about problem solving in the building of a bridge, siphoning at a water table, and painting a mural of a trip or about worksheets, numbers, letters, and predetermined tasks or projects.

Although we see our work and children through varied lenses, the adjustments necessary to bring varied parts into a focused whole are set personally. We juggle. We balance. Competing demands and perspectives create tension, leading to the inner dialogues that are an ever present part of teaching. In these ongoing conversations within self, unheard by others, we ask question after question. We wonder: Is the young child as egocentric as described by theory? Why is it so difficult to achieve a sense of community with this group? What's missing? Am I an observer and recorder of, or a participant in, development? What am I telling myself with my questions?

Just as I, the person teaching, am present in the choices I make and in the way I bring parts together to create a whole, each theory, each philosophy of education, has its own focus, its own story to tell about people and the world. If we turn to Dewey's philosophy of education, on what does he focus? What connections does he make? Who is the person who emerges from his vision? What story does he tell and to what kind of teaching will his story lead?

POTENTIAL AND CAPACITY

To find the person in Dewey's writings, we must leave behind the comfort and certainty of fixities, of detailed portraits, and give our attention to *potential* and *capacity,* to dynamic possibilities that require situations—a context—in order to be realized and made manifest. As Dewey notes,

> potentiality is a category of existence, for development cannot occur unless an individual has powers or capacities that are not actualized at a given time. But it also means that these powers are not unfolded from within but are called out through interaction with other things. (TI, 237; LW 14:109)

In a world that is ever ready to categorize and standardize, it may be difficult to think about teaching and planning for children in terms of potential and capacity, and possibilities.

Yet our lives with children, if we are open to possibility, hold surprises, those moments when a child exhibits understanding, a skill, or mastery we had not imagined he or she possessed. Each of us can remember an incident, a moment that gives reality and detail to the words "potential" and "capacity." What I remember vividly is six-year-old Michael. Although he became involved with materials, he was usually on the periphery of activity. Seldom was he chosen as a friend. In the energy and activity generated in a classroom of children, he was an awkward, background figure, an observer. Then there was the day in the school yard when a child grabbed another child's hat and threw it in the air. It landed on top of a seven-foot pole. Amazed, the children asked, "How can we get it?" Frustrated, the teachers answered, "Don't know." In the midst of the confusion Michael announced, "I'll get it." He shinnied up the pole, grabbed the hat, slid down gracefully, handed it to the owner and walked away. The awed silence was broken by cheers and numerous requests of "Michael, you want to play?"

The risk taking, the skill and prowess, the courage Michael exhibited in a few minutes were there but unknown to everyone. Michael had become a known, stereotyped by children and teachers. Potential and capacity were present, but no situation had offered the opportunity for their realization until those almost magical moments in the yard that changed his status in the group from that day on.

As with Michael, to find and know the person in Dewey's philosophy requires involvement with process, time, space, and histories, since forces and qualities remain lifeless unless elicited through interaction in the events and situations of the environment—an environment that exists, is there, while also is created and transformed through interaction. The person is "in" as well as "of" the environment. They are connected and continuous. Interacting with and in the social and physical environment of people and things, extended in time and space, elicits the person's capacity and potential. In each of these words Dewey finds a double meaning. While *capacity* may be defined as receptivity, Dewey chooses the connotation of "an ability, a power"; while *potential* may denote a dormant or quiescent state, Dewey chooses "potency, force" as its meaning (DE, 41; MW 9:46). Invariably, Dewey chooses meanings that highlight strength and possibility, especially the possibility for growth.

Turning to growth itself, Dewey notes that "the primary condition of growth is immaturity," and here, too, he converts what may be perceived ordinarily as a lack–immaturity–into a strength and power. In seeing immaturity as a primary condition for growth, and growth as a continuum, he attends to continuity and to the ability to grow. He does not compare the present, the immaturity of the infant/child, with what shall be in the future because then the child can only be seen as lacking. Deficiency and lack become primary when the present is seen not in itself but in comparison to a later stage, an end which then becomes a standard of measure for the present. Dewey locates the power and ability to grow in two words that he associates with immaturity–*dependence* and *plasticity*.

Without support, the physical helplessness of the human infant makes survival impossible. It is this dependence on others, the degree of helplessness, that suggests for Dewey "some compensating power." What enables the infant to cope with physical helplessness is to be found in the infant's social capacity–the power to involve others in self, to elicit interdependence, the infant's ability to evoke and facilitate social responsiveness. This is the strength, the power of the dependent immature infant.

As the infant interacts within the physical and social environment, adaptive actions and means are created, discovered, tried, modified, enlarged, and coordinated. It is these varied activities, this process of experimentation, that constitutes the infant's plasticity. By plasticity, Dewey does not intend softness awaiting imprint, but the ability to learn from experience. Plasticity is the power to retain from one experience that which will be of use in coping with the difficulties and newness of later situations. It is the ability to modify and coordinate actions on the basis of results gained in other experiences. As the infant acts on and in the environment, "in learning an action, instead of having it given ready made, one of necessity learns to vary its factors, to make varied combinations of them, according to change of circumstances" (DE, 45; MW 9:50). The infant learns not only momentary solutions that may be modified and reconstructed to meet the demands of unexpected and varied future situations, but also *how* to learn. In actively encountering and coping with the present, as actions yield consequences, means are created for meeting the future. With plasticity and dependence, the strengths Dewey finds in immaturity, he lays the foundation for two fundamental concepts in his educational philosophy: the social individual and learning from experience.

As Dewey's view of the person is detailed, the task of the teacher in relation to learning and development also emerges. If capacity and potential are realized in interactions with the environment, then the environments we create—the furnishing of space, the materials, the schedule, the social atmosphere—require special thought. If the children who enter the environments we create are not identified primarily by stages, as categories of development, scores, or pre/post something, but rather are seen as dynamic, unknown, storied beings ready to encounter and experiment, what environment do we create? What materials do we provide? On the surface, these may appear as simple questions but a more complex level exists. What kinds of interactions do I wish to support and promote? If the child is viewed as possibility, which possibilities do I support? What invitation do I wish to extend to children in the room I have created? Which qualities do I nurture? To what knowledge do I give priority? In what time-space shall being-becoming be experienced? On what do I base my choices?

With Dewey as guide, we enter a chosen domain. For all that has been and will be said about potential and possibility, Dewey has "preferred possibilities," those that promote a democratic society. Implicit in Dewey's philosophy of education, underlying the choices he makes and his view of the person, is his vision of a democratic society. Beginning with active, dynamic possibilities, what will be supported and encouraged in growth will be the qualities and predispositions that give life to and strengthen a democratic society. In describing the nature of the person, Dewey also is offering a guide to how such development—of the person and of a democratic society—may be realized. Intrinsically and dynamically related, self and society, organism and environment, must be examined together.

HABIT

Basic to understanding Dewey's story of the person is his concept of *habit*. It is a word Dewey used repeatedly and over time. In his writings on art, logic, philosophy, society, and education, he extended and refined the concept of habit as it was applied to a variety of circumstances. Its meaning became funded in being rotated and viewed from different settings. While the word *habit* may be an awkward and outdated word to use today in talking about people, it is essential to understanding Dewey's philosophy of education. We are accustomed to thinking of habit as actions that are repetitive, mechanical, routine, as our dichotomized "good" and "bad" habits. Although recurrence and rigidity are included within his broad definition of habit, the word as used by Dewey is the antithesis of the routinized, mechanical, and passive.

Habits are active, assertive, insistent, dominant, immediate. In *Democracy and Education*, habit is introduced as an expression of growth and is connected directly to plasticity, the capacity that enables us to learn from experience as we "retain and carry over from previous experience factors which modify subsequent activities" (DE, 46; MW 9:51). Within this process of trying and discovering, modifying and adapting, habits are formed and dispositions develop. Our habits—that is, our attitudes, inclinations, predispositions, sensitivities, and preferences—constitute and characterize the self. Our habits are the means by which we encounter and hold on to the world. For Dewey,

> The world we have experienced becomes an integral part of the self that acts and is acted upon in further experience. In their physical occurrence, things and events experienced pass and are gone. But something of their meaning and value is retained as an integral part of self. Through habits formed in intercourse with the world, we also in-habit the world. It becomes a home and the home is part of our every experience. (AE, 104; LW 10:109)

The world, this home, is inhabited by a self—an active, desiring, experimenting, interpreting, projecting being. Habits represent the selections we have made in our encounters with the environment, the choices that guide and lead our actions rather than the "bare recurrence of specific acts." Habits, our preferred modes of encounter and encountering, acting and interacting, are acquired, "seemingly instinctive," immediate, and "had." To be inclined, predisposed, speaks to the influence of prior activity, to preferences and meanings acquired over time. Habits reflect the continuity of self in time; they tell the story of our experiences and experiencing. Even when not used, habits are present in latent form in all that we do. Habits affect each other. They do not stand as discrete units of behavior or response. Habits interact and combine. They reinforce each other and interpenetrate. "Character is the interpenetration of habits. If each habit existed in an insulated compartment and operated without affecting or being affected by others, character could not exist" (HNC, 37; MW 14: 29–30). This effect of habit upon habit, the interpenetration of habits, creates integration and unity within the person. While we do not tend to use the word *habit* when we talk about children, Dewey's concept of habit is present in our conversations when we speak of a child's characteristic way of responding to situations, or when we recognize and are aware of how our predispositions, preferences, and inclinations contribute to the choices we make in teaching.

That habits are marked by continuity of attitudes and preferences might imply passivity, routine, or surrender—the person perceived not as having habits but as being had by them. Distinctions become necessary in order to maintain the dynamic, intentional character of habit. To distinguish between activity and relative passivity, Dewey introduces the word *habituation*. In our interactions with and in the world, we select those stimuli, situations, and events that we decide to take for granted, to accept just as they are, such as the routines with which we start each day—brushing teeth, bathing. In habituation, in our "enduring adjustments," the taken for granted provides leverage to our active habits. As Dewey observes, we are never interested in changing the whole environment. Habituation—the relatively unexamined and taken for granted—furnishes the background of growth, while habits constitute growing. Within this interplay of activity and relative passivity, habits can also become fixed, "habits that possess us instead of our possessing them" (DE, 49; MW 9: 54). In such instances, we have put an end to plasticity, that is, to the power to vary and to change, to see and respond with freshness, to our openness to the environment and to possibility.

With the focus on the emerging portrait of the person, little has been said about the environment. While the person has been described, the background has been taken for granted, a generalized, undifferentiated environment. Although this may serve as an illustration of active habits and enduring adjustments, it does not reveal the drama and dynamics of Dewey's thought. The person acts within and on an environment that is both stable and precarious, changing and durable, and always dynamically present. As Dewey notes,

> Breathing is an affair of the air as truly as of the lungs. . . . Seeing involves light just as certainly as it does the eye and optic nerve. Walking implicates the ground as well as the legs; . . . functions and habits are ways of using and incorporating the environment in which the latter has its say as surely as the former. (HNC, 17; MW 14:15)

As Dewey refines the concept of habit, a continuum appears. In our interactions with the environment, we have active habits, enduring adjustments, and habits that possess us. From infancy into childhood, a way of in-habiting the world begins and develops. Through our habits we encounter the environment of people and things. Our habits are our way of sensing the world, and making sense of the world, of being in it. As actors in the tragedies and comedies of living, we act on and within a changing stage. We assume different stances. At times we choose to stabilize the background so we can focus more fully on our actions. There are times when, for a variety of human reasons, we repeat ourselves and in repetition fix both our actions and the settings within which we act. And, we can also be open to and vitally present in the moment, seeing new meanings and possibilities in ourselves and in the setting.

Habit and Impulse

The classroom is a particular setting created by the teacher. We furnish the props and background. While the setting is always the present, the everyday, the past also is present in the yesterdays the children and teachers have lived and shared and in the stories and habits of each. We may think of the continuum of habits in terms of the environments we create, the invitations we extend, and our own teaching. The concept of habit can prod us to think about children's learning and also about ourselves. In the classroom worlds we create, how do we balance stability and change of the background in which children act? Are our responses born within the interactions of the present situation, or are they ready, repeated responses—habituated responses—that generalize the specific, thus diminishing potency and possibility?

An incident with a three-year-old may illustrate the difference between active habit and habituated responses in relation to language—those ready, familiar phrases we use daily, such as the frequently used "You need to . . . ," which begins many adult sentences. (Is it the child who "needs to . . . ," or is it the adult who needs the child to . . . ?) Sonny was an active child, full of ideas and energy. On this day he was a lunch server; his job was to give each child a plate. He placed a plate in front of the child sitting next to me and then, instead of placing my plate on the table, he hit me on the head with it. Stunned, I said, "We don't do that." With enthusiasm, Sonny instantly replied, "We didn't do it. *I* did it myself." Sonny's words were more stunning than his action. His words revealed the emptiness of the editorial "we." His honest and immediate response revealed the actual dynamics of the situation. He resisted the word that diminished his power. It was not a distant, generalized "we" who were involved but a "you" and "I," a Sonny and Harriet. My seemingly benign, habituated, and neutralizing "we" altered what had happened, and Sonny resisted that invisible control. Even though he knew his action was unacceptable, Sonny claimed his budding strength. In the process, he pushed me to question my language. He helped me to understand more deeply that no matter how similar, each encounter and situation has some newness, some difference, a uniqueness that requires particular attention, its own moment in time. Sonny's declaration and Michael's climb up the pole are not unique happenings. They are the stuff of daily classroom life, those moments that can transform our mind-sets and habits, opening them to change and possibility.

Common to the stories of Sonny and Michael is the element of surprise. In their interactions with the physical and social environment, each child responded in a manner that was unusual and unexpected. They unsettled habit through the novelty of their actions. It is in instances of energetic activity, of impulse and experimentation, that habits are reorganized. Impulses are the agencies of change, "for giving new direction to old habits and changing their quality" (HNC, 88; MW 14:67). Impulse is released when we encounter a novel, unexpected feature in our interactions with and in the environment, an encounter that unsettles established habits and initiates a change in the direction of our response to a situation or object. In the interplay between habit and impulse, sensation and impulse evoke and stimulate search and inquiry. They provoke unworded questions to which habits give form.

> Impulse defines the peering, the search, the inquiry. . . . Old habit supplies content, filling, definite, recognizable subject matter. . . . Without habit there is only irritation and confused hesitation. With habit alone there is machine-like repetition, a duplicating recurrence of old acts. With conflict of habits and release of impulse there is conscious search. (HNC, 169–170; MW 14:126)

Habits give form to and focus the unsettled by supplying recognition, judgment, and familiarity to the situation. And in such shifting of the accustomed and the novel, as "conscious feeling and thought arise and are accentuated," mind emerges. The evocative, catalytic nature of a problematic situation, the idea of conflict or disruption as a source for change and learning, is a recurring theme in Dewey.

In discussing impulse and habit, their relationship to stimuli, sensations, response, and consciousness has not been presented as simple associations or as being instances of direct, uncomplicated causation. For Dewey, sensations or stimuli do not stand alone—out there—happening to, or making an impact on, a merely registering organism, which then responds. The person determines, interprets, and makes sense of the stimulus. The sensation of light that evokes a response from the individual is neither mechanical nor simple. Rather, light stimulates the *act of looking*, a more complex undertaking of sensorimotor coordinations, of consideration given to the context in which action or stimulus occurs, and the presence of thought, intentionality, selection, and interpretation. Again, Dewey presents the individual as an active, mindful, determining person trying to make sense of and reconstructing a doubtful, uncertain situation.

A stimulus is all that is involved in "establishing the problem," the isolating of the source of conflict. Response becomes "the solution," a determining of a course of action that will settle confusion and restore continuity to experience.

The Social Nature of Habit

In the presence of so much individuality—of a responding, active person, meaningfully noting stimuli, selecting and transforming within events, mediating impulse and habit through conscious feeling and thought—one may well ask, where is the *social* individual? It is here that it must be remembered that habits are acquired, not native, and that their source is social. One must return to the physically helpless, dependent infant and remember that the infant's source of power is his or her social capacity, the ability to elicit the response of other persons and to initiate social interdependence. It is these social beginnings and connections that are the context within which habits are acquired and in which they become meaningful. It is in the social realm that habits, our paradigms, begin, are influenced, and are colored.

> To be influenced and guided by a paradigm is less a matter of knowing it as a series of rules or propositions, but rather is more a case of living it as an atmosphere of tacit meaning founded on the world-disclosing possibilities of pre-objective habit. In Dewey's terms, paradigms are had or lived before they are known—to have a paradigm is to have a habit. (Kestenbaum, 1977, p. 4)

It is in these infant beginnings that habits are formed, their formation shaped by culture, social surroundings, the relationships between and among people. Acknowledging the social origin of the evolving person, of the dominant role played by others in the formation of habit and character, it might be assumed that individuality is lost in the social, just as it might have seemed that the person's transforming, selective actions gave primacy to individuality. To tip the scale in either direction recreates a traditional either/or situation. From a Deweyan perspective, *social* and *individual* are not a question of balancing elements but a spatiotemporal affair of a whole that has "phases and emphases marking its activity." As Dewey presents the evolving person, the social and the individual may be said to be "two names for the same reality." It is not either the social or the individual but the *social individual,* each element functioning within the whole, named as separate elements for the purpose of analysis but in actuality transactionally related. Such a view ensures continuity and connections. It attends to process, time, and context.

Interaction and Transaction

Dewey's ongoing battle with polarized either/or conceptualizations requires that particular attention be given to language. He struggled to express new ideas with words already burdened with the inherent dualities, exclusions, and mind-sets he worked to transform. Over the decades, Dewey used the words *interaction* and *transaction* interchangeably just as the words *disposition, character,* and *attitude* became other names for habit in many of his writings. To understand the social individual and the extent of the connectedness between person and environment that Dewey intended, it is necessary to attend to language and to make certain distinctions.

A fundamental difference between interaction and transaction is that the former speaks to the action of separate entities. Transaction shifts emphasis from separations to transformations, from action between to action within, and gives primacy to the occurring situation.

> From a transactional perspective, an "element" is a functional unit that gains its specific character from the role that it plays in the transaction. From this perspective it is the transaction that is primary. A transaction does not occur with an aggregate or combination of elements that have an independent existence. On the contrary, what counts as an "element" is dependent on its function within a transaction. (Bernstein, 1966, p. 83)

From a transactional perspective the social individual is an organic whole. This precludes a hierarchical ordering of elements or independent, disconnected parts added together to create a whole. Rather, within an organic whole transactions occur between the functional elements of "social" and "individual," between the preferred, acquired, remembered, and the new, original, novel. As situations bring these elements into interplay, they act, and in action, transform themselves and the situation in which they occur. That situations invariably are required in order to elicit or provoke action and transformations does not signify an unusual or special occurrence. It is to state the natural course of events. The person is a being-always-in-a-situation. And in situations, elements and their surround do not lie inert and lifeless; contact creates and evokes tensions and movement, and gives rise to selective actions in search of significance.

COMMUNICATION AND COMMUNITY

How do things, events, objects, interactions come to possess meaning? We begin our lives within a culture. We begin with others; we are associated. We enter into a present in which language exists.

> Of all affairs, communication is the most wonderful. . . . When communication occurs, all natural events are subject to reconsideration and revision; they are re-adapted to meet the requirements of conversation, whether it be public discourse or that preliminary discourse called thinking. Events turn into objects, things with a meaning. They may be referred to when they do not exist, and thus be operative among things distant in time and space, through vicarious presence in a new medium. . . . Events when once they are named lead an independent and double life. In addition to their original existence, they are subject to ideal experimentation: their meanings may be infinitely combined and re-arranged in imagination and the outcome of this inner experimentation—which is thought—may issue forth in interaction with crude or raw events. (EN, 138; LW 1:132)

Language is the means by which we affect each other and ourselves in contemporaneous dialogues—within self and with others. Language is the "how" of our connectedness, the way in which we come to possess things in common. Communication requires partners who each will modify and regulate their activities in order to secure understanding.

> Such is the essence and import of communication, signs and meanings. Something is literally made common in at least two different centers of behavior. To understand is to anticipate together, it is to make a cross-reference which when acted upon, brings about a partaking in a common, inclusive undertaking. (EN, 148; LW 1:141)

To "anticipate together" requires the ability to see self from the perspective of the other and to respond to the situation from the standpoint of the other. In perceiving a thing or situation "as it may function in (another's) experience, instead of just egocentrically," we modify and regulate our actions (EN, 148; LW 1:141). The cooperative partnership involved in significant communication requires a reaching out, a towardness, to see self as seen by others and, in the desire for understanding, to use this additional perspective as a regulator and modifier of one's own behavior. It is to see the world through the eyes of the child and to try to imagine how the child may see us, which may be quite different from the way we think we are presenting self.

Just as language makes implications possible in events, turning them into objects with meaning, communication between partners makes it possible to see self as "other" and from such a view to project consequences. Inner dialogue becomes a ground for shifting action, refocusing, and reinterpretation. Just as impulse may shift focus and unsettle habit, thus leading to change, the ability to see self from the perspective of another in communication becomes a means in the search for meaning and understanding. Communication is both means and end.

There is more than a verbal tie between the words common, community, and communication. Men live in a community in virtue of the things which they have in common; and communication is the way they come to possess things in common. What they must have in common in order to form a community or society are aims, beliefs, aspirations, knowledge—a common understanding—like-mindedness as the sociologists say. . . . The communication which insures participation in a common understanding is one which secures similar emotional and intellectual dispositions—like ways of responding to expectations and requirements. (DE, 4; MW 9:7)

It is not "bare association" that will endow significance or meaning to a community, nor mere physical proximity. It is the sharing of activity. It is in doing together, in the sharing of hopes and aspirations, in participating toward a common end that communities are created and sustained. When Dewey uses "like-mindedness" in talking about community he does not intend the identical, or the absence of individuality, for community is not fixed or static. It is vital and dynamic. It is like the social individual. It has constants that give it stability and it also has movement, change, and transformations brought about by the participation of individuals. The common, the shared, is not a perpetuation of the present unchanged. Society and community do not carry themselves; they are maintained and changed by collective and individual action. Beside the common and the shared must be placed the unique, the novel, the unexpected, the unknown, the element of freshness that is the hallmark of individuality. It is individuals acting and selecting—exercising choice—that introduces change and readjustments.

Speaking of community in terms of oneness is misleading, for it may imply homogenization, whereas, in actuality, a community is made up of individuals with membership in diverse groups—of family, of class, of race, of gender, of religion. It is when these different memberships, with their varied perspectives, can be interwoven into a fabric of shared meanings and aspirations that community is born—when each person making his or her unique contribution participates in an undertaking meaningful to each and inclusive of all. For Dewey, the community that supports such movement and existence is a democracy. It "is a way of life controlled by a working faith in the possibilities of human nature" (CD, LW:14, 226).

A democracy is more than a form of government; it is primarily a mode of associated living, of conjoint communicated experience. The extension in space of the number of individuals who participate in an interest so that each has to refer his own action to that of others, and to consider the action of others to give point and direction to his own, is equivalent to the breaking down of those barriers of class, race, and national territory which kept men from perceiving the full import of their activity. These more numerous and more varied points of contact denote a greater diversity of stimuli to which an individual has to respond; they consequently put a premium on variation in his action. They secure a liberation of powers which remain suppressed as long as the incitations to action are partial, as they must be in a group which in its exclusiveness shuts out many interests. (DE, 87; MW 9:93)

Potential and capacity require an environment that invites realization, and individuality is fostered in a community that celebrates plurality as a means for renewal. Diversity extends the scope of community, enlarges and elaborates its meanings. The transaction within the individual between preference and novelty, interest and surprise, also carries over to community in its efforts to maintain a common base of meanings within a structure that is sufficiently permeable to permit the entrance of new and enriching possibilities. Just as plasticity is the power which permits habits to change, permeability offers openings for revitalization and growth.

Creating Community

An analogy may serve to bring together what has been said about communication, shared activity, common purpose, and the social individual. The words Dewey chose to describe or explain his ideas on these varied topics created a particular image that served as a background of understanding. The image was one of theater and drama as he spoke of settings, action, and qualities. In *Experience and Nature,* as Dewey discusses the function of language, he states,

And soliloquy is the product and reflex of converse with others; social communication an effect of soliloquy. If we had not talked with others and they with us, we should never talk to and with ourselves. . . . Through speech a person dramatically identifies himself with potential acts and deeds; he plays many roles, not in successive stages of life but in a contemporaneously created drama. Thus mind emerges. (EN, 141; LW 1:135)

While the analogy of life as drama is not uncommon, Dewey's presentation leads to thinking of drama in a particular way—as the work of an ensemble. An ensemble consists of individuals who come together to create a whole, and that which binds them in unity is what they share and do together. A shared common purpose permeates, colors, and directs doing. In a true ensemble roles are rotated. Today's lead may appear tomorrow as a supporting player. Choice depends on ability and personal contribution. This openness of position, that is, whether one may lead or support, act or direct, extends to envisioning new possibilities for self, to the trying of new forms of participation.

The use of talent—one's potential and capacities—becomes an open affair, as situations spark experience into unexpected pathways. The sharing of the whole by each contributing member, the communication of all aspects of shared doing, serve to clarify and strengthen purpose. Communication becomes a means of including others in our process and activity, an opportunity for others to become familiar with and a part of our view of the whole. We become catalysts for each other. Shared communication offers to each member the opportunity to gain multiple perspectives as one tries to understand the concerns and visions of each member—both as a unique individual and as a functioning member of the group. The spirit of an ensemble is not an overnight affair. It depends on the participation, the undertaking, and the willingness of each member. It includes the giving of self to the work of which all are a part. The success of accomplishment is the result of multiple transactions, of giving and transforming, of receiving and being transformed. The shining moment of any one contributor holds within it the touch, the thought, the caring of each member of the ensemble and is a success shared by all. It is not a selfless giving or contributing. Self is not lost in joining and sharing with others. It is extended.

For a spirit of unity to exist within an ensemble we must add the factor of time—time to define purpose, to share activity, to experiment and to risk, to learn from success and failure, to open up each other's possibilities. The unity created by an ensemble grows out of its history. The cohesion of the whole does not result from a magnetic core that attracts and adds to create itself but from the potential force of individual parts coming together to create their own magnetism from which a whole is then realized.

Whose script is being played? The idea of an ongoing script, a play "in production" with certain consummate moments, phases, and emphases, and no final curtain, matches Dewey's view of growth and the absence of absolutes and final endings. It allows room for the entrance and exit of cast and new undertakings along with planned, familiar presentations and remembered forms. It is experimental theater, and as such, requires sustained effort and caring to succeed. And to that must be added faith in what one is doing and in each other. And for a sense of community to exist for a group of children and their teacher, within the disparity of age and power that exists, there must be trust. Trust that as I, the learner, risk into the unknown—experiencing the vulnerability that comes invariably with change and learning—my efforts, my searching will be met with caring and support.

RELATED READINGS

Isaacs, S. (1972). *Social development in young children*. New York: Schocken Press.

Rogoff, B. (1990). *Apprenticeship in thinking: Cognitive development in social context*. New York: Oxford University Press.

Wersch, J.V. (Ed.). (1985). *Culture, communication and cognition: Vygotskian perspectives*. New York: Cambridge University Press.

3

The Social Individual in an Early Childhood Setting

The immediate and direct concern of an educator is then with the situations in which interaction takes place. The individual, who enters as a factor into it, is what he is at a given time. It is the other factor, that of objective conditions, which lies to some extent within the possibility of regulation by the educator. . . . The phrase "objective conditions" covers a wide range. It includes what is done by the educator and the way in which it is done, not only words spoken but the tone of voice in which they are spoken. It includes equipment, books, apparatus, toys, games played. It includes the materials with which an individual interacts, and most important of all, the total social *set-up* of the situations *in which a person is engaged*.

(EE, 45; LW 13:26)

The children who enter our classrooms, as noted above, are who they are at any given time. Viewed through a Deweyan lens, to a large extent what they are tends to be unknown. That is, accepting Dewey's premises, children have potential and capacity. They come with habits, habits that make them storied beings. They have their own ways of being and of doing. Through language and custom they are connected to and associated with others. They bring with them memories of their interactions in the physical and social environment and their questions about those worlds. What Dewey offers us are possibilities about people rather than detailed portraits. Through our interactions we will come to know detail and tell it in our stories at the end of each day. To the possibilities Dewey offers, compatible detail may be added from developmental theory—from Vygotsky, Piaget, Isaacs, and others—but with the caution that while adding detail we make certain to leave sufficient space for unknowns, for what the children shall make of, and realize, with what we offer. We must be aware, too, that we not commit what Dewey called the "psychological fallacy": "the confusion of experience as it is to the one experiencing with what the psychologist makes out of it with his reflective analysis" (CE, 165; MW 1:118).

As we begin to translate theory into practice, to what sources do we turn? Theories of development offer us a view of development, of how children grow, how they learn generally or in specific knowledge areas. What such theories do not offer us is *what* is to be learned or *why* it is important to learn it. Even though, at times, the *what* of curriculum may be inferred from developmental theories, they do not inform the *why* of our doing. In Dewey the educational *why* is interwoven in the view he presents of the social individual. As noted in Chapter 2, Dewey's educational philosophy grows out of his vision of a democratic society. Translating this philosophy into educational practice requires thinking about the development of both a democratic society and its citizens. The realization of each involves the other.

For the teacher a framework for decision making is offered. Will what I am planning encourage and support the just and inclusive perspective necessary to a democratic society? What will be the consequences to a growing sense of community if I choose to do *this* rather than *that*? Which helps me to create the social atmosphere and participation conducive to communication, to developing shared interests, to promoting associated living? As I think of community, what space have I created for diverse voices, for interactions between and among various groups? What opportunities have I offered children for the experimentation, the novelty, that will give rise to new visions, questions, and meanings that may challenge the unexamined, the stereotypic in thought and feeling?

As we review our aims and consider the various developmental domains—the "whole child"—a larger vision and ideal are interwoven into a Deweyan perspective. What we know and understand about children is influenced by what we hope the children will become: people in whom "I" and "we" are not either/or polarities but constituent, essential elements of self; for whom responsibility and caring are inclusive concerns; and for whom active participation and struggle to achieve a just society are a way of life. In acknowledging our participation in and contribution to the direction of growth, what we also accept is our responsibility to be vitally present in the moment of teaching as well as being conscious of the consequences of our actions, which cannot be left to chance or be mechanical or routine. We are asked to keep active habits of critical intelligence alive and to maintain an attitude of anticipation, of openness and questioning. Be it the realization of potential or community, each remains in the realm of possibilities that coexists with chance and contingency. While we know that possibility and the hoped-for do not come with guarantees or certainty, we choose to speak and act with commitment to what we value and work to realize in our teaching, to the ideals we responsibly choose for guidance. In consciously choosing, we are acknowledging also that teaching is not value free, that a transactional relationship, a reciprocal informing, exists between aims and means, between process and product.

CREATING THE PHYSICAL ENVIRONMENT

Few of us have had the opportunity to teach in classrooms where from the start we had a voice in deciding where shelves will be placed, what type of tables we will have, or where clothing cubbies will be built. Usually, we begin in rooms where such decisions about space and furnishings have been made. As we look around, we wonder: Do these arrangements extend the invitation I wish to offer? Guided by our view of children and our aims, we look at physical space and imagine varying scenarios. "And this is where we can have meetings each day . . . if I move these tables to the side." "There'll be more room for the children to use the math manipulatives if I move them to this shelf. Yes, then they can work in small groups on the rug or on the table." "Will this cause too much traffic near the writing area? Too much noise?" "Where will we put the cots if those block buildings stay up?" On and on we imagine scenes of activity, snatches of future realities, that match what we would like life to be in this space where we will live daily with children

To articulate how space is to be used, that is, to state the kind of living to be encouraged among the people who use it, anchors thoughts and feelings in reality. We can imagine and desire a myriad of activities occurring in our classrooms and while so engaged we may easily stretch imagination, and walls, to accommodate each new possibility. Yet, faced with a room that is actually 30 by 20 feet in which there are 25 children, one must make choices while dealing with the unyieldingness of plumbing features and doorways. The choices we make, the physical and social arrangements we create, reflect our philosophical grounding.

From what has been said of the transactional relationship between the child and the environment, it is clear that within a Deweyan framework the classroom environment demands primary attention. Environments consist of people and things as well as space itself, and each must be considered. From the philosophical framework that has been created, based on Dewey's assumptions about the nature of the person and the concept of community, the fundamental function of the physical space of the classroom is twofold: to create those conditions that will evoke each child's potential and capacity, and, further, will facilitate interactions that promote and encourage the communication necessary to create community. To realize these aims, the physical environment would promote

Free movement and activity. In addition to the fact that action is necessary to interaction, freedom of movement makes it possible for us to gain knowledge of the children with whom we work. "Enforced quiet and acquiescence prevent pupils from disclosing their real natures. They enforce artificial uniformity. They put seeming before being" (EE, 62; LW 13:39).

Associated living and shared activities. "In place of a school set apart from life as a place for learning lessons, we have a miniature social group in which study and growth are incidents of present shared experiences. Playgrounds, shops, workrooms, laboratories not only direct the natural active tendencies of youth, but they involve intercourse, communication, and cooperation—all extending the perception of connections" (DE, 358; MW 9:368).

MATERIALS: CONSTRUCTING KNOWLEDGE OF SELF AND WORLD

The materials we choose to bring into the space of our classrooms reveal the choices we have made about knowledge and what we think it is important to know. How children are invited to use the materials indicates the role they shall have in their own learning. Materials are the texts of early childhood classrooms. Unlike books filled with facts and printed words, materials are more like outlines. They offer openings or pathways by and through which children may enter the ordered knowledge of the adult world. Materials also become tools with which children give form to and express their understanding of the world and of the meanings they have constructed. If materials are tools for learning and means for obtaining knowledge, which materials are chosen to equip the early childhood classroom becomes a matter of significant consequence.

Although considerable variation exists in the appearance of early childhood programs, there are certain materials that have become staples. It is here that a further qualitative distinction must be made. Why a material is chosen and the kinds of learning opportunities it is seen as offering are basic considerations. For example, manipulatives and paints are standard equipment in most programs for young children. If a teacher chooses these materials based primarily on thinking such as "because they are part of the early childhood curriculum" or simply "because children enjoy the activity," then thinking remains on the surface, on acceptance of conventions that remain unexamined.

If, on the other hand, a teacher articulates that working with a particular material may create opportunities for symbolic representation, social and language development, problem solving, and social studies content, and may support the development of a sense of community, then much more thought will be given to space allocation, to quantity and arrangement of materials, to the supplementary activities needed to support and facilitate such learnings. In themselves materials only create an opportunity. The kind of opportunity it will become, the quality of experience to be had, requires further reflection and articulation. The depth and scope of a teacher's understanding of the potential of a material and where it may lead determine the quality of a child's experience with the material. Choosing materials requires more than familiarity, more than liking, more than unexamined acceptance of the ubiquitous presence of a material in every classroom we have known.

To what choices does Dewey's philosophy lead when a teacher considers materials? Are there criteria to guide in the selection of materials and their use? The two considerations stated for evaluating space – the possibilities for activity and sociality – remain fundamental. The materials to be chosen would build on this foundation by extending to children an invitation to be active participants and by promoting communication and association within the group. What follows is an illustration of how a philosophical framework, in this instance based on Dewey's thought, serves as a basis for decision making. It is an illustration of how fundamental ideas and concepts are brought together to form a foundation for decision making in thinking about children, curriculum, and teaching. It is to say: How do I concretize an aim – what is valued – so that it is visibly present or sensed in the very atmosphere of the classroom? And in this instance it is to ask: How do Dewey's concepts of the social individual, of habit, of community and communication come alive? What is offered are possibilities, ways of thinking about theory and practice and ends and means from a Deweyan perspective. A different philosophical framework would give priority to other criteria, to choosing other materials and activities.

While eliciting the child's active participation, materials and activities help the child to learn how to learn, making learning an activity of the self. To do so, the material should challenge the child by eliciting ideas and posing problems, and by serving as direct sensory stimuli that may unsettle predispositions and attitudes, and should be sufficiently varied in use to allow for unique rather than standardized responses. Activities that would meet this criterion are those in which questions or problems are posed for the child to pursue and research. Discussions in a variety of subject areas, such as science, math, literature, and social studies, bring questions about the world to the surface, leading to active experimentation and discovery. Open-ended questions are followed with, How can you find out? What do you think will happen if you . . . ? The contrast is with tasks that are preset and directed step by step and in which there is little room for the messing about, the experimentation, that elicits personal interest and connections.

While eliciting the potential and capacity of the child, the materials offered also help the child to recognize his or her own strengths and power. To do so, the material would be available to the transforming action of the child and allow the child to perceive the impact of his or her action. For this to happen, the material should have sufficient character in itself—an identity with properties with which the child must contend. In essence, the material should be sufficiently plastic to become a tool for experimentation, while also maintaining its essential nature, which thus makes it a substantive partner in inquiry. Also, a material may be experienced as a statement of reality. Wood presents a durable, relatively unyielding nature. Water offers fluidity, wetness, and transparency. In the encounter and engagement with materials, qualities of and ways of experiencing and relating to the environment are found.

While offering the child novelty and challenge, materials and activities also reflect the familiar and experienced world of the child. To do so, materials should have some connection with the child's world as lived. Some degree of continuity exists which connects the present with established meanings and thus arouses interest. Known materials such as water, sand, and paper, among others, may acquire new dimensions and be viewed differently as they are encountered in new contexts of use. And in the puzzles, games, and books available in the classroom, connections to and images from the child's world and culture will be present and visible. And it is here, as connections are made between the child's past and present, between the familiar and the new, between home and school, that openings are created for the presence of family members in the classroom. Inviting children's families to come and share their interests, skills, and knowledge lessens the distance children may feel between their personal and public worlds.

While grounded in the familiar, materials and activities also invite active exploration of the world beyond the classroom and family. To do so, many opportunities will be offered for play, for conversations, for children's personally rooted questions growing out of their lives. The world outside the classroom is not a separate world; the two are connected. In dramatic play children construct their worlds literally and symbolically. Their play reflects what is known and what is imagined. Dramatic play often raises new questions that need further exploration of and in the environment. Discussions and trips are necessary to enlarge perspective, to expand and clarify connections, to understand interrelationships, to provide information, and to help children make sense of the world in which they live. Also, activities such as planting and cooking, which in themselves offer varied opportunities for math, science, and language, also serve as catalysts for children's research on and in the larger environment.

While expanding the world beyond the known and the familiar and providing variety and challenge, the materials and activities offered are in themselves means for the expression and communication of one's thoughts and feelings to self and others. To do so, materials would be varied in nature so that a range of textures and forms is available to children for the communication and expression of things known and felt—means that in their diversity reflect the variety of experiencing and imagining—the realm of qualities, intangibles, and unknowns, as well as the concrete, the actual, and the "at hand." For example, as noted earlier, the hard, unyielding three-dimensionality of wooden blocks is like the angular and impenetrable found in the world, while the malleable three-dimensionality of clay may express the softness and pliability also present. Such materials also require the user to make choices. When working with these unstructured materials, children must select from the whole of experience those aspects to which they wish to give form, to express and communicate to self and to others. Choice is present in terms of the content to be declared and also in how best to realize this statement through the material. Similarly, movement, painting, and the writing of stories growing out of trips and events in the room also are examples of activities that may offer opportunities for expression and communication.

While offering opportunities for choice and continuity in experiencing, and the communication and transformation of experience, the materials and activities chosen encourage associated activity—the sharing with others of ideas, activity, purpose, and meaning. To do so, the materials selected will be sufficiently flexible to accommodate the activity of one child or the participation of many. It is in materials and activities that lend themselves to sharing ideas, to utilizing common space and objects, to encouraging communication among participants, to generating varied functions in work, that a sense of community and shared purpose emerges and a democratic vision begins.

Whenever there is conjoint activity whose consequences are appreciated as good by all singular persons who take part in it, and where the realization of the good is such as to effect an energetic desire and effort to sustain it in being just because it is a good shared by all, there is in so far a community. The clear consciousness of a communal life, in all its implications, constitutes the idea of a democracy. (PIP, 149; LW 2:328)

If materials are viewed as the texts of early education, then choices must be made in relation to materials and knowledge. What knowledge is valued? From a Deweyan perspective, what is chosen to study, to learn, "is to be considered as a means of bringing the child to realize the social scene of action" (MPE, 31; MW 4:279). It is social studies—the interconnecting of various disciplines—that gives primacy to the social individual, to learning about human effort within its spatiotemporal context, and offers opportunities to introduce and examine ideas about interdependence, diversity, change, and connectedness. The appeal of social studies lies in the possibilities it offers to view the experiences of people, past and present, from diverse perspectives. Means are offered for understanding and finding meaning in the continuity of nature and the dynamic relationship between people and their environment. As Dewey notes in a discussion of geography, one of the disciplines within social studies, "the ultimate significance of lake, river, mountain, and plain is not physical but social; it is the part it plays in modifying and directing human relationships" (MPE, 34–35; MW 4:280–281). Social studies is an opening for questioning and making sense of the social and physical world of our interactions, an ever-widening spiral of learning and understanding about self and world—whether the focus is a three-year-old's interest in self and family, a five-year-old's study of jobs in the community, or an eight-year-old's research on recycling or the history of the original settlers of an area.

In stating these criteria and offering detail in terms of materials and activities, the connection between the *what* and the *what for* of curriculum is made visible. Also present is Dewey's view of the organic relationship between ends and means.

> Means and ends are two names for the same reality. The terms denote not a division of reality but a distinction in judgement. . . . "Ends" is a name for a series of acts taken collectively. . . . "Means" is a name for the same series taken distributively. (HNC, 35; MW 14:28)

From such a perspective ends and means, the "what" and "how" of our doing, are transactionally related. The end becomes an end-in-view. "It is no longer a terminal point, external to the conditions that have led up to it; it is the continually developing meaning of present tendencies—the very things which as directed we call 'means'" (EN, 302; LW 1:280).

Structured and Unstructured Materials

The attention given to materials and activities is not to be understood as pertinent primarily to the lower range of early childhood. They are also important in the primary years where experimentation and the construction of knowledge still depend in large measure on the personal, the concrete, and the informing of thought in and through action. Unstructured materials and open-ended activities resemble in nature the person as described by Dewey—potentiality, possibility, and realization through interaction.

The repeated return to unstructured materials as exemplars does not cancel the importance of other materials. There are values to be found in a variety of the structured and semistructured materials used in early childhood programs: puzzles; peg boards; manipulative games matching shapes, size, and color; math manipulatives; Montessori materials; lotto, dominoes, and other games. The structure and specificity of such materials lead to the acquisition of valued and significant skills such as fine motor and eye/hand coordination, sensory discrimination, understanding part/whole relationships, and concept development. As such, they have a real place in the curriculum. At the same time, the narrower scope of their possibilities that are inherently present because they have an intended, predetermined purpose, does not make them as fully available to extended, unique interactions. For example, a child may do a variety of things with puzzle pieces—use them as "people" in an imagined dramatic sequence or arrange them in a pattern on the table—but basically a puzzle sets the task of fitting pieces together within a frame to re-create a predetermined whole. Further refining distinctions among materials, the colored, wooden one-inch cubes found frequently in early childhood programs are less structured than puzzles. In comparison with scaled building blocks, which vary is shape and size, one-inch cubes are more structured, offering fewer possibilities for the expression of ideas and feelings.

True acceptance of the uniqueness of each individual will acknowledge that not every person is ready, willing, or eager to face the challenge of unstructured materials at all times. There is comfort and reassurance to be derived in having the challenge preset on occasion. For some children, the existence of a preset purpose enables them to concentrate more fully on the task at hand and also may serve as a springboard for reaching out toward unstructured possibilities.

Whether materials are structured or unstructured, whether activities are open-ended or directed, is not a question of balance between two poles. Adults can structure the most open-ended material by directing its use, and children can open up the most structured materials by the free use of their imagination. More to the point in determining choice is intentionality. Knowing the children with whom I work – their attitudes, predispositions, and preferences – what multiple opportunities can I offer to enlarge their world and abilities? What variety of choices – genuine and meaningful – can I offer so that they may approach their questions and interests from various perspectives? Is "we" a dynamic, growing community that welcomes the freshness and vitality of diverse "I's"?

Asking such questions brings us back to our educational aims, what we hope to realize, for it is there that we ground and determine our choices. Whether we select structured or unstructured materials, open or directed activities, what is asked is that we observe carefully to understand what the situation requires, remembering that situations, for Dewey, consist of the interaction between the child and the environment. If there is to be genuine engagement, whatever we choose, it must be meaningful to the child. And for situations to evolve, to evoke, to be, there is a further factor to consider: time.

TIME

How children will approach and use materials is determined in large measure by how we conceive of time. How time is perceived greatly affects the nature and quality of children's experiencing in the classroom. Schedules reveal as much about our purposes as do room arrangements. The two – time and space – are intrinsically connected in the planning and decision making of the teacher. Together, they reveal adult attitudes concerning knowledge, human nature and interactions, authority, control, and the locus of power. How time is perceived is influenced by personality, culture, and society. Time may be experienced as pressure or expansion; it may be perceived as measure or as perspective. It may be seen as rhythm or cycle. What we decide to do with the time of children and their time with us, reflects what we consider meaningful and significant. The language in which time is described – as allowed, used, given, taken, lost – tells as much about attitudes as do the words used by teachers to describe their function in relation to students' written work, which may be approached as something to grade, mark, correct, or read.

Understanding Children's Conception of Time

Adult conceptions of time, the flash of digital numbers or the movement of clock hands from hour to hour, do not hold great meaning for young children. Although they imitate adult phrasing and ask for "five more minutes" or announce that "in two days it's my birthday," these remarks are a sharing by the child of acquired adult conventions and phrases. They are an exercise in and the practice of the use of social forms of ordering rather than accurate statements of understanding. The experiencing of time, necessary to understanding its nature and function, requires participation in and awareness of its passage. The interactions possible in several years of living are insufficient to enable the young child to abstract from the whole of experience temporal categories and segments. For children time is fluid, its flow accented or eased by inner states. How the adult enters into that movement, with or without understanding or acknowledgment of its subjective source, affects children's growing understanding of the concept of time. It also affects and shapes how they respond to their inner cues. In these invisible interactions between children and adults a great deal is learned about power, of powerlessness, and of being empowered. As Dewey observed, the formation of enduring attitudes, which he termed "collateral learnings," is often the more important learning gained in schools rather than the specific lessons of subject matter (EE, 48; LW 13:29).

Time is a favored topic of authority. Questions such as "when are you scheduling . . . " and "how much time will be used in . . . " often make time a commodity to be spent effectively and efficiently, something to be filled rather than experienced. The qualitative may become secondary, if not lost, by the pursuit of quantity. Although Dewey did not speak specifically of daily schedules, he did attend to time. In an implied sense, time is present as background to all that Dewey addresses in education in his concept of growth. Further, with potentiality—that which requires the existence of interaction in order to be realized—time is a necessary factor. The realization of potential requires movement: the activity of interaction and the passage of time, and it includes the presence of possibilities, qualities, and individuality. The passage that follows comes from an essay by Dewey, "Time and Individuality."

> Individuality conceived as temporal development involves uncertainty, indeterminacy, or contingency. Individuality is the source of whatever is unpredictable in the world. . . . To say this is not arbitrarily to introduce mere chance into the world. It is to say that individuality exists; that individuality is pregnant with new developments; that time is real. . . . The mystery of time is thus the mystery of the existence of real individuals. It is a mystery because it is a mystery that anything which exists is just what it is. We are given to forgetting, with our insistence upon causation and upon the necessity of things happening as they do happen, that things exist as just what they qualitatively are. We can account for a change by relating it to other changes, but existences we have to accept for just what they are. . . . Genuine time, if

it exists as anything else except the measure of motions in space, is all one with the existence of individuals as individuals, with the occurrence of unpredictable novelties. Everything that can be said contrary to this conclusion is but a reminder that an individual may lose his individuality, for individuals become imprisoned in routine and fall to the level of mechanisms. Genuine time then ceases to be an integral element in their being. Our behavior becomes predictable because it is but an external rearrangement of what went before. (TI, 239–241; LW 14:111–112)

Contained in this passage is a great deal that is of concern to teachers, in how we will conceive of time and of the opportunities for learning that we create for children. It is we, in creating that "most important total social set-up" in the classroom, who determine whether time will be a possession of the participants or something by which they are possessed. The phrasing of the previous sentence is similar to earlier statements about habit. The resemblance is neither accidental nor superficial. Habit becomes involved in the discussion of time and individuality as Dewey himself elicits the connection between the two in the above passage when he contrasts genuine time with "external rearrangement of what went before," and as he considers instances when individuality becomes imprisoned in routine and is reduced to the mechanical. The immediate message for teachers is the importance of approaching each classroom situation with freshness and to avoid the ease and comfort derived from repetition, routine, and habituated responses. Also brought into the discussion is our

responsibility for understanding the needs and capacities of the individuals who are learning at a given time. It is not enough that certain materials and methods have proven effective with other individuals at other times. There must be reason for thinking that they will function in generating an experience that has educative quality with particular individuals at a particular time. (EE, 45–46; LW 13:27)

As we plan learning opportunities, using a Deweyan framework requires that we think about the realization of children's potential along with their predispositions and attitudes, and the habits through and with which they uniquely encounter situations. Included in our thinking is the time children need to frame their own questions as they seek understanding of self and world. The unstructured materials cited so frequently are truly unstructured and able to provide the opportunities indicated when they are available within a time frame that allows for experimentation and for the repeated use that encourages depth in understanding. What is asked is respect for the fluidity of children's conception of time, and the honoring of their genuine immersion in its flow.

Scheduling

With such awareness and understanding, it becomes important to think about a schedule that makes it possible for children to work without many interruptions and transitions from one activity to another. Nonfragmented stretches of time not only give children the opportunity for more in-depth involvement and experimentation, but also allow room for situations to evolve, to become meaningful in a way that they may not be at first glance. Within stretched time, greater possibility exists also for making choices and for experiencing the consequences of one's doing. Such an approach requires that time be viewed as perspective, as rhythm, as opportunity, and that the present moment be valued fully.

The philosophical grounding that Dewey offers also would draw our attention to consider the need for time shared with others, for working and talking together, for finding and exploring common purpose. Coming together as a group would not be left to chance. The schedule would include definite times when children and adults come together as a community—to see, to sense, to communicate their groupness. This would be in addition to individual time as well as times when small groups work together using materials, or in activities such as graphing, cooking, reading, and searching for needed information. An observation made in the 1970s when American education was influenced greatly by the British infant schools is pertinent here. At that time many teachers in the United States adopted some of the classroom practices, room arrangements, and materials found in the British infant schools. Among the imported practices was the setting up of a juice/milk table for midmorning snack to which the children went in their own time. This was in contrast to children stopping their work and coming together for snack. With time, some teachers, especially those interested in creating a sense of community, realized that the gain of having fewer transitions brought with it the loss of a communal, shared time. Coming together as a group for snack, children and adults could listen to and participate in multiple and diverse conversations—talk about the accomplishments of the morning ("Two more people to ask and then we do the graph."); plans for the next activity ("You want to make the design together?"); stories about happenings outside of school ("It rained. You know where we had our picnic? On the kitchen floor!"). In an informal group time, sitting together, sharing food and talk, one had the opportunity to experience self among others. A seemingly small scheduling matter had within it much larger philosophical implications.

And as we think of scheduling, it is important to remember that time also is present in the concept of habit. Habit, as stated earlier, "is influenced by prior activity and in that sense acquired." It is "projective, dynamic in quality, ready for overt manipulation" and operative in "subordinate form" even when not "obviously dominating activity" (HNC, 39; MW 14:31). A distinction was made between active habits and those which no longer remain open to possibility, becoming routinized and fixed. A further refinement of habit was presented in those instances in which one effected a "persistent response," a background of "enduring adjustment." Within this continuum of active, relatively passive, and fixed attitudes, the significant factor to be considered is the effect of each on plasticity—the ability to learn and to grow. Just as habituation creates a stable background for active habits, a daily schedule for young children requires some standard, expected features that offer the structure from which children may then improvise. That is, within the wholeness of the day, children know that there are certain constants that exist, guarantees of the presence of certain events. These constants serve to mark the passage of time. They make possible the vocabulary of "before," "after," "during," and "while." Outdoor time, room time, lunch time, reading time, are the watches of young children. These consistently repeated events help to regulate and stabilize the day, freeing children to give themselves to the invitation of materials and activities. They may commit themselves to their work and trust that such commitment does not mean missing lunch or story.

The question then becomes: What parts and how much of the program are to be considered "constants"? It is possible to carry a principle beyond its purpose and usefulness to serve other ends. There are schedules that are boringly predictable, created not to support children's efforts but to enable adults to go through the day with a minimum of effort and protected against the possibility of encountering novelty. The appearance of such smoothly flowing routine with everything going "as it should" can also be the very place where plasticity has been hardened, where unique inner agendas have become molded into stereotypic forms, and possibilities converted into predetermined expectations.

What has been said of habit and of time pertains not only to children and their learning but also to the adults working with them. We are asked to be consciously aware of our own plasticity and to be open to "taking a chance," to being available to the vulnerability involved in learning. Acceptance of the view of human nature offered by Dewey brings with it a degree of unsettlement for teachers. We cannot depend on stock responses; we cannot function with standardized expectations. We cannot plan exactly how something will turn out. Phrased positively, what we are asked to include in the planning of curriculum, if it is to be congruent with this view of the person, is the expectation that there will be diversity in responses, space created for the unique contributions of participants without knowing exactly what those contributions will be, and awareness of the possibility that factors may enter the situation that will alter its course. Growth in a Deweyan sense is a lifelong process of continuous construction and reconstruction, of the transformation of experience, a lifelong process for children and adults.

RELATED READINGS

Biber, B. (1972). The "whole child," individuality and values in education. In J. R. Squire (Ed.), *A new look at progressive education* (pp. 44–87). Washington, DC: Association for Supervision and Curriculum Development.

Cuffaro, H. K. (1991). A view of materials as the texts of the early childhood curriculum. In B. Spodek & O. M. Saracho (Eds.), *Issues in early childhood curriculum* (pp. 64–85). New York: Teachers College Press.

Isaacs, S. (1966). *Intellectual growth in young children.* New York: Schocken Press.

King, N. R. (1992). The impact of context on the play of young children. In S. A. Kessler & B. B. Swadener (Eds.), *Reconceptualizing the early childhood curriculum: Beginning the dialogue.* New York: Teachers College Press.

Mitchell, L. S. (1934). *Young geographers.* New York: Bank Street College of Education.

4

Children and the Curriculum

We always live at the time we live and not at some other time, and only by extracting at each present time the full meaning of each present experience are we prepared for doing the same thing in the future. This is the only preparation which in the long run amounts to anything.

(EE, 49; LW 13:29–30)

Permeating all that has been said about space, materials, and time is the centrality of the activity and participation of children in the entire undertaking. What must be underlined is that their participation is to be understood as more than the taking of what is offered; it must include their contribution to the whole. Children, along with the adults with whom they work, are curriculum creators. Teachers create learning environments by selecting materials, arranging rooms, considering time, thinking about and coming to know the interests and concerns of children. We organize activities and plan possibilities that will elicit and support these interests and that will extend and move them into richer learning and experiencing. As just described, emphasis falls on the child's partaking of what is offered by the teacher. For the situation to be what Dewey intended, the child's contribution must be clearly evident. Without it, all that has been said about potential, possibilities, and realization remains merely words. What teachers create is a setting with props and the outline of a script. The outline is a necessity for otherwise criteria would not exist for the selection of props or the creation of the setting. The outline cannot contain all the events and situations that will occur, the conversations that will take place, or the detail of the transactions that will eventuate in this setting. The contributions of the children cannot be known without their presence. And here again we must guard against creating an either/or situation. The large contribution of children to the content of curriculum does not cancel the teacher's contribution in the same domain. Both are dealing with the same thing but approach it from different perspectives. The child's entry is personal, vital, and qualitative, derived from his or her experience and immediate concerns. In *The Child and the Curriculum,* Dewey vividly describes this personal world of the child.

> The child lives in a somewhat narrow world of personal contacts. . . . His world is a world of persons with their personal interests, rather than a realm of facts and laws. Not truth, in the sense of conformity to external fact, but affection and sympathy, is its keynote . . . the child's life is an integral, a total one. He passes quietly and readily from one topic to another, as from one spot to another, but is not conscious of transition or break. . . . The things that occupy him are held together by the unity of the personal and social interests which his life carries along. Whatever is uppermost in his mind constitutes to him, for the time being, the whole universe. That universe is fluid and fluent; its contents dissolve and reform with amazing rapidity. But, after all, it is the child's own world. It has the unity and completeness of his own life. (CC, 92–93; MW 2:274)

To think of the child as a contributing participant to the developing curriculum requires the existence of several basic assumptions. First, although the child's world is more personal and narrow, this does not mean that the child resides in a world other than the one in which studies and subject matter exist and have been organized. They are one and the same. Second, the transitory nature and the fluidity of children's interests do not make these interests less valid or less connected with the organized world of studies. Further, that the interests of the child "are held together by the unity of the personal and social interests which his life carries along" does not mean that in being personally rooted they are divorced from, or devoid of, the content of subject matter. Denial of any of these assumptions is to make the child a stranger, a being outside human history and endeavor. The acceptance of these assumptions still leaves the question open of how to connect the particular with the general, the fluid with the organized, the personal and the objective.

In large measure the connection is made possible by understanding that the two are "in" and "of" each other, that the subjective and the objective are constituent elements of a situation, transactionally related. It is from such a perspective that the entry point for the teacher is found. It is the teacher who has access to both worlds, who has come to know and understand both "constituent elements" of the situation, the world of the child and the field of studies. Teachers thus become the link that bridges the personal world of the child and the larger, ordered world of categories, of impersonal facts and laws, and logical classifications. With our broader perspective and experience and our panoramic view of the educational undertaking—a perspective impossible for the child—we create the means for bridging and connecting. We do so through the opportunities for experience that we offer—space, materials, time, and our genuine attention.

CREATING ORDER IN TRAFFIC AND WITHIN SELF

An anecdote highlighting the dramatic play of a kindergarten group in the block area over a two-week period in late autumn may serve to synthesize and also to indicate some additional areas requiring the teacher's consideration. There are 25 five- and-six-year-olds in the group. In terms of space allocation more than a third of the room has been devoted to the use of blocks and dramatic play. Also in the room are manipulative materials, woodworking, clay, painting, drawing, writing, reading and math activities, and cooking. At the beginning of the week when building began in the block area, about 11 children decided to work there. At a group meeting, they stated the type of buildings they intended to make and also whether they were going to work alone or with others. By this time in the year they knew that their buildings would stay up over the course of the week.

By Tuesday morning, when this anecdote begins, seven of the original builders were in the area. The other four were busy in other areas of the room—two at the workbench, one painting, and the other looking at a book about firefighters—but they remained connected to the work in the block area. The structures were a police station, a hospital, a circus, a fire station, a castle, a pizza store, a playground, and two homes. Among all these buildings, a complicated network of roads had been built for cars. Some of the roads had no real destination in that two led directly into a wall and one ended abruptly between two houses. Neither situation seemed to disturb the children.

Tuesday

The teacher observes that two children have started racing cars on the roads, with a police car in hot pursuit. They bump into a building. It is the pizza store of one of the racers, who shouts, "It's O.K.!!" and they continue to race. Other children in the area stop working to watch the chase. A fire fighter joins the race making a loud siren sound. The teacher makes a general announcement, "Please be careful of people's buildings."

Wednesday

Before children go to work there is a brief meeting at which the teacher notes that the car racing on the previous day had caused the knocking over of part of the pizza store. The pizza store owner says, "That's O.K. I'm going to change it to a gas station."

As children begin working in the area, the car racing begins again, with greater speed than on the previous day, both on and off the road. The teacher walks over to the area and stands there in a prominent, obvious spot. This does not deter the racers, who in time accidentally crash into the hospital. The loud crash brings other children to the area, including the builders of the hospital, who are shouting, "You better fix that!!" As most of the children have gathered in the area, it turns naturally into a meeting.

TEACHER: People's buildings are being knocked down. We have to talk about that. What's happening?
HAROLD: They knocked down our hospital and they better fix it!!
TEACHER: How did that happen?
PETER: Well, you see I had to get away. They were chasing me and I was running and the building was in the way.
ELLEN: You should looked where you were driving.
PETER: I was too.
TEACHER: Right. Now, what was the chase all about?

Several children respond at once. "The police had to catch the bad guys." "There were robbers." "I'm not a robber. I was going fast to help."

TEACHER: Wait a minute. We can't understand when everyone talks at once. There were robbers? Were the police chasing them?
RONNIE: But the police started the chasing today. The police aren't supposed to do the robbing work.
HAROLD: Yeah. The police are supposed to make the traffic good and they give tickets. My uncle got one. He parked wrong.
TEACHER: Well, what can we do here? Some people are worried about their buildings.
MARIA: The police could give tickets to people who don't stop in the light.
ELLEN: And people who go too fast.
HAROLD: And if you don't park good.
TEACHER: O.K., what shall we do?
JOE: We'll give tickets. Peter and me are the police.

TEACHER: When will you give tickets?
JOE: Well, if somebody is going too fast, the police car will go to
          them and say, "Stop! You have a ticket." And I'll give them
          one. You know, a piece of paper.
ELLEN: Remember, YOU don't go fast.
PETER: (mumbling) To catch them I do.

Several tickets are given out in the remaining work period.

Thursday

More children than the original 11 are working in the block area.
After about 20 minutes, many children hold tickets, some the proud
possessors of four or five. The two weary police officers, Joe and Peter,
complain, "They all got tickets. They're not listening. It's not fair. We
better talk." The teacher calls the whole group, saying that Joe and Peter
have something important to say to everyone. They state the problem.
Ticket holders recount with pleasure how they received their tickets. It is
obvious that getting a ticket is not a deterrent but the beginning of a
prized collection.

LAURIE: The police have to stop them. That'll be a rule.
JOE: But nobody listens. They like the tickets.
KAREN: Maybe when you get a lot of tickets you can't drive no more.

This causes considerable interest and the children finally decide that after
receiving three tickets the person will no longer be allowed to drive. The
police will keep count. By the end of the morning there are only two
children left who have not been grounded. It rains in the afternoon and
the children remain indoors. Some go to the block area to work. There are
no cars on the road. The ambulance from the hospital rushes to the castle
to pick up a patient.

Friday

The morning meeting begins.

TEACHER: Today is Friday and we'll be picking up later today. Does any-
          one in the block area have anything to say? Any announce-
          ments?
PETER: It's no fun. Nobody can drive anymore.
RONNIE: It's your fault. You go too fast.
PETER: Shut up, stupid. I'm the police.

TEACHER: O.K. This is really very hard for everyone. What can we do?
KAREN: We could have a school. Maybe some people go too fast be-
          cause they don't know how to go slow. They could learn.

There is silence as the children think about what Karen has said. David
asks, "Is our school a driving school?" There is some discussion as to
whether the oldest children in the school are allowed to drive. Gradually,
the discussion turns to What do you have to know in order to drive? As
the children state it, "What are the rules?" Within that context the teacher
states that there are driving tests to be passed and uses the word *license*,
which is now incorporated into the discussion.

Karen announces that she will build a driving school. Ronnie and
Susie join her. Among the rules that must be learned, as decided on in the
discussion, are: (1) Stop on the red light; (2) Watch for children in the
street; (3) Pay attention with your eyes. A chart is made of the rules and
taped on the wall near the driving school.

Second Week

Beginning on Monday, Karen, Ronnie, and Susie build a driving
school again. Gradually, a format seems to evolve. Two kinds of clients
come to the school. One group is composed of those children who bring
their wooden block "people" to the school and announce, "I don't know
how to drive." The others arrive with "I lost my license." Activities related
to the driving school remain central for the entire week and provide the
content for many discussions.

As the children became involved in their own dramatic play content
and as they included new information, many questions came up. Some
questions were primarily information seeking. How old must you be to
drive a car? Can grown-ups really lose their license for driving too fast?
What color is a license? What does a license say on it? Other questions grew
out of the experience of the dramatic play in the block area, as when Ellen
asked, "Is it safe to walk in the street?" It took some probing to understand
the real meaning of her question, which was: If the person who is driving
the car is just learning to drive, how safe is it for pedestrians? There was
enormous relief when the teacher mentioned that driving school cars are
clearly marked. And as Peter reassured Ellen, "That's why the car has that
sign. So when you see that sign you keep a mile away around the car." He
stretched his arms to indicate the mile. Following that discussion a small
group went out to an intersection to observe traffic and to look for "driving school cars." A humorous carryover from this whole experience was a
comment made several weeks later by an exasperated child whose building

had been bumped into repeatedly by another. She said, "You do that one more time and you're going to lose your walking license!"

REFLECTING ON THE EXPERIENCE

The children's contributions to curriculum are evident in this anecdote. They contributed to content, direction, timing, and organization. The teacher contributed perspective and the creation of a framework into which elements could be interwoven. In sharing the development of curriculum, both teacher and children participated in the construction of knowledge and the direction of study as partners in the undertaking. The children had the time in which situations could evolve, producing dilemmas with which they had to contend. The children's questions and comments were rooted in their own experiences. They were given form by the activities in the block area and then connected in various ways to the larger world. Karen's contributions brought order and hope to difficult situations. Peter's own struggle with control was evident in his shifting positions in play: initially a police officer; then a dual-role racing officer; then issuing tickets for racing; finally, reassuring Ellen and himself through the rules he helped to create and the information he had incorporated.

Themes and individual questions appeared and reappeared over the year, the time children needed to make sense of their experiences and to incorporate new information. Different situations rotated questions so that they could be seen from a different perspective and in varied circumstances. Encounters with other children dealing with similar themes brought confrontations and differing views of reality. The teacher, in her clarifying, generalizing, focusing function, and through leading questions and comments, served to link personal worlds with the larger world. She supported the emergence of a shared perspective. As representative and voice of the group, the teacher helped the children to see situations from the perspective of others ("some people are worried about their buildings"). The teacher tried to help children recognize the connection between actions and consequences. And Karen broadened everyone's perspective when she introduced the importance of understanding the complexity of human behavior in her reassuring observation that "maybe some people go too fast because they don't know how to go slow."

The children achieved a sense of groupness through the community they created out of the common interests and work they shared in the block area. This sense of community carried over to other areas and activities. In varying degrees, each child experienced being a significant part of the group. Identity consisted of uniqueness and of partnership with others. Community did not cancel individuality. Personal concerns often became common concerns; individual questions became topics of discussion to which each child could contribute his or her thinking and assessment. The acquisition of skills, information, and knowledge was an ongoing endeavor shared by all in discussions and in working together. Over time the children became participants in each other's knowing.

> To be a recipient of a communication is to have an enlarged and changed experience. One shares in what another has thought and felt and in so far, meagerly or amply, has his own attitude modified. Nor is the one who communicates left unaffected. . . . The experience has to be formulated in order to be communicated. To formulate means to get outside of it, seeing it as another would see it, considering what points of contact it has with the life of another so that it may be got into such form that he can appreciate its meaning. Except in dealing with commonplaces and catch phrases one has to assimilate, imaginatively, something of another's experience in order to tell him intelligently of one's own experience. All communication is like art. . . . Any social arrangement that remains vitally social, or vitally shared, is educative to those who participate in it. (DE, 5–6; MW 9:8–9)

In this multiple sharing, the complex and loaded questions of control and of authority—flattened, depersonalized, and made antiseptic in being labeled "classroom management"—take on new form and meaning. Seeing authority and control as a two-sided matter, open to both sides, alters the situation. It becomes, as Dewey noted, "not the will or desire of any one person which establishes order but the moving spirit of the group. The control is social but individuals are parts of a community, not outside of it" (EE, 54; LW 13:33). When the source of authority and control shifts to being a social process, when children are seen as a social group rather than the objectified *class*, "the situation changes drastically. The teacher loses the position of external boss or dictator and becomes the leader of group activities" (EE, 59; LW 13:37).

THE MORAL IN THE CLASSROOM

Inherent in what has been said about the nature of the person, the interrelationships among people in community and communication, and social control, there is an implicit attitude, a tone, infusing the whole. For Dewey, education is a moral undertaking and his view of the moral, as might be expected, is organic and focused on action in context. The moral is not a separate, idealized domain. It is present in and a part of everyday living. Dewey does not offer absolutes or idealized models for guidance when discussing the moral. The person is not seen as a follower of "givens" but as an active agent of intelligence and imagination who in interaction with the environment responds with preferences and sensitivities, who reflects, analyzes, and makes choices. Dewey's focus is on process, on how we make ethical choices in the situations that provoke deliberation and that culminate in a value judgment. Situations that provoke deliberation are those in which we face a choice between or among competing courses of action. Faced with a dilemma, the need to choose, we engage in a deliberative process to determine the action to be taken. In our deliberation we create and try out different scripts, we rehearse the consequences that will follow. Thinking and feeling, we choose and ascribe value. In discussing Dewey's moral theory, Rucker (1972) makes a distinction between principles and rules, a distinction particularly pertinent to classroom living.

> Principles are general ideas arising out of experience as guides for experience; they are tools for dealing with new situations, methods for solving problems. A rule, on the other hand, is like a recipe, a set of specific steps to follow to attain a fixed end; and ethics cannot provide moral rules because each concrete problem is different from every other, and all moral problems are concrete ones. Moral theory, just as any theory for Dewey, is an intellectual tool, not a body of achieved knowledge in which he can rest. (p. 115)

For Dewey, questions of the "good" are not a matter of the given or *the* good, for "good" is a located good. It is good-in-this-context because later experience may reveal weaknesses in the process of valuation that led to determining the present good. Or new factors and situations that were not originally present may appear that affect and influence present judgment. For Dewey, valuation is an ongoing search not for stable ends but for informed, meaningful living. Over time, through experience and continued reflection on experience, values and standards emerge from deliberation. They serve as principles to guide action, but as every present offers "something more" that may affect applicability and relevance, principles, too, must be revaluated.

For the teacher, concern with the moral requires the adoption of an attitude, a perspective, an approach. It means to be aware that the moral is present in every interaction, in all instruction, in every aspect of classroom life. The "moving force" of ideas means that actions taken must be action-reflected-on. And *must* appears because reflection is the assumption of responsibility for the consequences of actions taken, their effect upon self and others. A moral perspective is not an *addition* to the existing curriculum but intrinsic to, and growing out of, classroom life.

We need to see that moral principles are not arbitrary, that they are not "transcendental"; that the term "moral" does not designate a special region or portion of life. We need to translate the moral into the conditions and forces of our community life, and into the impulses and habits of the individual. . . . The one thing needful is that we recognize that moral principles are real in the same sense in which other forces are real; that they are inherent in community life, and in the working structure of the individual. (MPE, 58; MW 4:291)

In the anecdotal material presented in this chapter children had many opportunities for choice and deliberation and the possibility to extract moral ideas from the situations they created in their dramatic play. Children had the time and repeated opportunities to assess, formulate, and communicate their view of a situation, to state what they valued, and to encounter the values of others. Within the community of the classroom created by the teacher, the children created their own community in play and within that structure confronted practical situations and conflicts that were personally meaningful and relevant. In the simplicity and concreteness of the situations they created, dilemma and choice became manageable. Ethical questions and thinking came within their reach.

Consideration of the moral in education involves more than deliberation. The qualitative must also be considered. There must be an "emotional reaction," a "delicate, personal responsiveness."

Indeed, good judgement is impossible without this susceptibility. Unless there is a prompt and almost instinctive sensitiveness to conditions, to the ends and interests of others, the intellectual side of judgement will not have proper material to work on. Just as the material of knowledge is supplied through the senses, so the material of ethical knowledge is supplied by emotional responsiveness. (MPE, 52; MW 4:288)

To understand emotional responsiveness, the qualitative, it is necessary to look more closely at the interactions of the social individual and to examine *experience* in its variety and detail.

RELATED READINGS

Cuffaro, H. K. (1984). Dramatic play–The experience of block building. In E. S. Hirsch (Ed.), *The block book* (pp. 62–78). Washington, DC: National Association for the Education of Young Children.

Donaldson, M. (1978). *Children's minds*. New York: W. W. Norton.

Scales, B., Almy, M., Nicolopoulou, A., & Ervin-Tripp, S. (Eds). (1991). *Play and the social context of development in early care and education*. New York: Teachers College Press.

5

Experience: Variety and Continuity

"Experience" denotes the planted field, the sowed seeds, the reaped harvests, the changes of night and day, spring and autumn, wet and dry, heat and cold, that are observed, feared, longed for; it also denotes the one who plants and reaps, who works and rejoices, hopes, fears, plans, invokes magic or chemistry to aid him, who is downcast or triumphant . . . [experience] recognizes in its primary integrity no division between act and material, subject and object, but contains them both in an unanalyzed reality.

(EN, 10; LW 1:18)

Experience is a word found frequently in the talk of early childhood teachers. We talk of children manipulating objects, of sensorial exploration, of activity, and of "learning from experience." Words that become part of a professional vocabulary can, with time, become thin, their meaning stretched beyond usefulness. As a teacher of teachers, when I have asked, "What does it mean to learn from experience?" the question is often met initially by a perplexed silence soon broken, quite often, by explanations of how "children learn by doing." It takes much probing, the telling of many stories, the recalling of memories of childhood accomplishments to arrive at some understanding of the complexities involved in the simple phrase "to learn from experience." As the phrase is so closely connected to Dewey's philosophy of education, what does he mean by the word *experience*? How does he connect experience with learning? What detail can the word *experience* add to the story, the portrait, of the social individual?

If a word count were ever done on Dewey's writings, the word *experience* would reign supreme. Experience is Dewey's way of seeing the world and the human condition. With experience as the lens through which he sees, anything he touches will be connected to people, to their lives and concerns. Focusing on experience as constituted of the interactions between the person and the environment, Dewey is able to confront and transform ancient dualities. Person and nature, subject and object, knowing and doing, mind and body all become connected rather than polarized when experience is the vantage point for reflection. The view from experience affords a vista of organic wholes, of continuities, process, and situations.

Dewey's concept of experience has "phases and emphases" marking its development. There are many "definitions" of experience to be found in Dewey's writings. Each statement offers yet another shading, an additional nuance on which to reflect. To grasp the fullness and richness of the concept requires that it be viewed both panoramically and in close-up. The larger view furnishes constants and essentials; the particular distinguishes phases and emphases of the whole.

RESPONDING TO QUALITY AND CONTEXT

In the previous chapters the center of concern was the nature and development of the social individual. Experience—"an affair primarily of doing," of what people do and suffer, "strive for, love, believe and endure"—was presented in broad strokes, as the very process of living, the myriad events and moments that constitute human biography and history (EN, 10; LW 1:18). It is in looking at the variety in life and living, the *what* of experience, that distinctions appear within the whole. In the transactional relationship between person and environment the world is encountered in multiple ways. Examining the variety of these encounters discloses both the *how* and *what* of experience, and the human search for meaning, remembering that

> the realm of meanings is wider than that of true-and-false meanings; it is more urgent and more fertile. . . . Poetic meanings, moral meanings, a large part of the goods of life are matters of richness and freedom of meanings, rather than of truth; a large part of our life is carried on in a realm of meanings to which truth and falsity as such are irrelevant. (EN, 332; LW 1:307)

Meaning is not out there, fixed, outside of self, waiting to be discovered or delivered. Like mind and self it is achieved, attained, through action and within a context, a situation.

Much of human experience and experiencing is ordinary. A large portion of our living is of the everyday, unnoteworthy variety characterized by "distractions and dispersions," "starts and stops." In beginnings of such everydayness, experience may be transformed into affairs of knowledge and of consummation. To understand such movement, notice must be taken of the element common to experience in all its variety—the existence of quality. The world in which we immediately live, the world of our daily striving, is "preeminently a qualitative world. What we act for, suffer, and enjoy are things in their qualitative determinations" (QT, 176; LW 5:243). It is how we respond to quality that makes experience what it is and determines the direction it will take.

For Dewey, qualities are "immediate," "had," "felt," "things directly possessed," existences unavailable to discourse. Awareness of the immediacy and ineffability of qualities does not mean that we have entered a mystical domain. Qualities are "unknown and unknowable," not because they are remote or obscured "behind some impenetrable veil of sensations or ideas, but because knowledge has no concern with them" (EN, 73; LW 1:74). It is here that a fundamental point is made about experience and knowing. Dewey is stating that the immediacy of qualities—that they are had, possessed directly—is not to be equated with immediate knowledge. The immediacy of having is not to be confused with immediate knowing. What one "has," "what one feels," is quality; it is not knowledge. Experience is not always, or primarily, "an affair of knowledge." Knowing requires words, descriptions, explanations, connections, ordering. Qualities, immediate things, "may be *pointed to* by words, but not described or defined" (EN, 73; LW 1:75). And there is much in experience that is not involved primarily in knowing.

Reference to the qualitative may be mistakenly understood as indicating certain rare and heightened moments of existence. On the contrary, rather than being special, for Dewey the qualitative world is the very world that we experience daily. It is the world of our transactions with the environment. Qualities are in the situations of transaction. To be "in" in such an instance does not connote "in" as "marbles are *in* a box" or as "paint is *in* a can," as Dewey notes on various occasions. "In" refers to the interaction or transaction; it is not a reference to placement or distinctions, for qualities are neither in the person nor in the environment. Qualities are in the situation because the person is alive and present, dynamically interacting in and on an environment. It is in our analyses, in our attempts to define and to explain with words, that we locate or classify qualities as being subjective or objective, or as belonging to mind or matter. "The qualities never were 'in' the organism; they always were qualities of interactions in which both extra-organic things and organisms partake" (EN, 212; LW 1:198–199).

A situation itself is marked by an all-pervasive quality, a quality that permeates "all the objects and events that are involved." A situation is the field in which objects and events are experienced; no object or event stands

alone, isolated, unrelated to a context. It is the all-pervasive quality that
unifies and binds the constituent parts of a situation into a whole. Again,
we are in the presence of the nondiscursive, for situations in their qualita-
tiveness "cannot be stated or made explicit." A situation is "taken for
granted"; it is "understood" (QT, 181; LW 5:247). All-pervasive quality is
not a property added to the situation. It is there because the situation
exists as it is constituted. For example, in his essay "Qualitative Thought,"
Dewey notes that a person may respond to a painting by saying it is the
work of a particular artist or by someone influenced by that artist. The
person passes that "judgement long before he has made any analysis or any
explicit identification of elements. It is the quality of the picture as a
whole that operates" (QT, 195; LW 5:259). Analysis may determine the
elements contributing to this quality but analysis is an act of, an objectify-
ing, a coming after the immediate *having* of quality.

It is here that habit re-enters the discussion because it is habit, "the
net outcome of prior experiences," that gives a "dominant quality" to
our perceptions. Habits—our attitudes and predispositions, that which
is shaped and formed in previous experiences—produce an "immediate
reaction." Habits are the means by which quality is sensed, felt, or had. It
is with and through our habits, endowed as they are with prior meanings,
that we grasp the quality in a situation. It is what we do with quality, once
it is felt, that determines the direction of experience. In encountering
quality our response may be fragmented or surface, we may be fully present, or we may respond with confusion and uncertainty. Each of these
responses to quality are openings to different kinds of experience and
experiencing, distinctions that are pertinent to the educational implications of Dewey's concept of experience.

Dewey's concept of experience also requires that attention be given to
time, for experience stretches. It is serial, an "affair of histories." Experience—the transaction between the individual and the environment—is
marked by phases and emphases, by rhythms of encounter and withholding, of beginnings and endings. Time is necessary if experience is to stretch,
to infer, to become what we make it to be in our transactions with the
environment. It is consideration of this passage in time, what we make of
our living time, that discloses the variety in experience and its transformations. And included in the temporal aspect of experience there is Dewey's
consistent attention to context, to relations that qualitatively bind objects
and events into specific and connected *this* thing, *that* happening. Experience is a spatiotemporal affair.

In the "general stream of living" the quality that dominates and characterizes a situation may be disrupted by the manner of our response. We
fragment experience when we remain on the surface of interaction, when

we "undergo sensations as mechanical stimuli," or when "we see without feeling," or touch "but the contact remains tangential" (AE, 21; LW 10: 27). And when our response to a situation is one of bare recognition, we arrest the possibilities of a situation and of our experiencing. Dewey makes a sharp distinction between recognition and perception.

> The difference between the two is great. Recognition is perception arrested before it has a chance to develop freely. In recognition there is a beginning of an act of perception. But this beginning is not allowed to serve the development of a full perception of the thing recognized. It is arrested at the point where it will serve some *other* purpose, as we recognize a man on the street in order to greet or to avoid him, not so as to see him for the sake of seeing what is there. (AE, 52; LW 10:58–59)

Recognition is a falling back on habit without plasticity, where the present moment is identified by fitting it into a "previously formed scheme," a convenient stereotype. The contrast is with situations where recognition passes into perception—an act of reconstructive doing—when consciousness becomes "fresh and alive." In perception we actively participate; we study and take in. In phrasing reminiscent of the interpenetration of habits, Dewey adds further detail about perception when he states:

> *This* act of seeing involves the cooperation of motor elements even though they remain implicit and do not become overt, as well as cooperation of all funded ideas that may serve to complete the new picture that is forming. Recognition is too easy to arouse vivid consciousness. (AE, 53; LW 10:59)

In the too-facile neat matching of the present to the past that comes with mere recognition, there is not enough "resistance between new and old to secure consciousness of the experience that is had" (AE, 53; LW 10:59). In moments of preoccupation with other matters, we withdraw from our surroundings by withholding our receptivity. These are the "starts and stops," "the dispersions and distractions" in experience. We make experiences "anesthetic" when we hold back, or drift through events without connecting, when we respond in a "slack and humdrum" manner. In such doing, though we have touched the qualitative, we side-step the aesthetic potential in experience, the possibility of fulfillment.

AESTHETIC EXPERIENCING

Clarity, wholeness, intensity, completeness are hallmarks of those experiences in which the aesthetic potential is realized, when we speak of having *an* experience.

In such experiences, every successive part flows freely, without seam and
without unfilled blanks into what ensues. . . . In an experience, flow is from
something to something. As one part leads into another and as one part
carries what went before, each gains distinctness in itself. The enduring whole
is diversified by successive phases that are emphases of its varied colors. . . .
Because of its continuous merging, there are no holes, mechanical junctions,
and dead centers when we have *an* experience. There are pauses, places of
rest, but they punctuate and define the quality of movement. They sum up
what has been undergone and prevent its dissipation and idle evaporation.
(AE, 36; LW 10:43)

With these words, Dewey is not describing moments in life that come
heralded by the clarion call of angels. He is talking of events and situations
as ordinary as finishing a piece of work in a way that is satisfactory, solving
a problem, playing a game of chess, eating a meal, carrying on a conversation, taking part in a political campaign (AE, 35; LW 10:42). The ordinary
becomes noteworthy when the situation or event "is so rounded out that
its close is a consummation and not a cessation" (AE, 35; LW 10:42).
Such experiencing possesses rhythm, wholeness, and unity, the person
fully present in a situation. To be fully present speaks to the interpenetration of habits, the giving to a situation of an interconnected self (for habits
constitute self) in which accrued prior meanings heighten the present and
there is anticipation of the developing form of experience. Such experiencing is like art in that "it celebrates with peculiar intensity the moments in
which the past reenforces the present and in which the future is a quicken-
ing of what now is" (AE, 18; LW 10:24).

The re-enforcement of present by past is through habit that retains
meaning from prior experiencing. Meanings are what we come with to a
situation. They are our immediate, pre-reflective, sense-giving linkage to
the world and the continuity of self. In experiencing that is aesthetic there
is a coming together within self—an integration of emotions, meanings,
and body—so that none predominates but each is vitally present. In a
situation where present qualities fuse into an all-pervasive quality, in the
transaction of self-in-a-situation, there is the rhythm of encounter, of
development, of fulfillment. Here there are no starts and stops, but merging and fusing. There are no distractions and dispersions, no tangents, but
a rhythm that leads toward unity. It is the very nature of the world in
which we live with its tensions, obstacles, and struggles that makes completion and fulfillment possible.

Because the actual world, that in which we live, is a combination of movement and culmination, of breaks and re-union, the experience of a living
creature is capable of aesthetic quality. The live being recurrently loses and

reestablishes equilibrium with his surroundings. The moment of passage from disturbance into harmony is that of intensest life. In a finished world, sleep and waking would not even be distinguished. In one wholly perturbed, conditions could not even be struggled with. In a world made after the pattern of ours, moments of fulfillment punctuate experience with rhythmically enjoyed intervals. (AE, 17; LW 10:22–23)

While the above passage speaks of re-establishing equilibrium, the harmony or balance that Dewey seeks is dynamic rather than static or mechanical. The attainment of equilibrium marks the beginning of a new relation to the environment. "The time of consummation is also one of beginning anew" (AE, 17; LW 10:23).

INQUIRY AND THE INDETERMINATE SITUATION

Within the rhythm of breaks and re-unions, and of achieved harmony in living, emphasis also may fall on the problematic in experience. It is such experience, involving inquiry and knowing, that has received the greatest attention in connecting experience and education. Dewey contributed to this unbalanced view of experience with his detailed, fully explicated analysis when writing about experience and education in relation to reflection and inquiry. Something is offered that is tangible. In several of Dewey's books, particularly his educational writings, the reader may find a step-by-step outline of a process that bears a variety of labels—reflective thinking, the process of inquiry, the scientific method, the problematic situation. In the detail and explication offered, the process is almost "packageable," available to becoming a technique, a step-by-step procedure to be followed. To approach inquiry in such a manner is to strip the process of its nuances, its qualifications, and its intrinsic connectedness with other concepts—quality, habit, situation. Skeletal outlines and mere step-by-step procedures ultimately deny the relationship of the process to the person's experience. It becomes something outside the flow of experience and personal meanings. From such a perspective, the process may be easily construed as an approach fitting to all experience. To do so is to assume that knowledge and reason are what experience is all about, whereas Dewey's point is that knowing is but one aspect of experience.

In both experiencing and thinking there are phases and emphases, distinctions and demarcations to be found. While thinking is present in daydreaming, reverie, fleeting impressions, and random recollecting, Dewey's concern is with reflective thinking, which includes imagination and recollection. How does Dewey characterize this type of thinking? In *How*

We Think he begins his discussion quite simply as he observes that reflective thinking "is the kind of thinking that consists in turning a subject over in the mind and giving it serious and consecutive consideration" (HWT, 4; LW 8:113). In *Democracy and Education* the general is detailed and elaborated, as Dewey notes that "thought or reflection . . . is the discernment of the relationship between what we try to do and what happens in consequence. No experience having a meaning is possible without some element of thought" (DE, 144–145; MW 9:151). And further:

> Thinking, in other words, is the intentional endeavor to discover specific connections between something which we do and the consequences which result, so that the two become continuous. Their isolation, and consequently their purely arbitrary going together, is cancelled; a unified, developing situation takes its place. The occurrence is now understood; it is explained; it is reasonable, as we say, that the thing should happen as it does. (DE, 145–146; MW 9:152)

It is evident in both passages that reflection includes intentionality and ordering. It is a process that necessitates the presence of a conscious self ordering and examining experience purposefully so that it may become unified and meaningful. The unity and wholeness characteristic of the aesthetic experience now is pursued consciously and achieved through deliberate effort. If living, experiencing, is not to be left to chance, to random possibilities, to repeated trial and error, then thought is necessary. Through reflection the present is projected into the future as we consider the consequences of our actions. In making connections through reflection, we direct experience with purpose. In our anticipated projections, we direct experience toward transformation, toward restoring connections to that which has become indeterminate, unsettled.

Action and thought are not two discrete aspects of experience. It is not to undertake an activity and then at its end to contemplate the results. What is stressed is that the two must not be separated, for each informs the other.

> To "learn from experience" is to make a backward and forward connection between what we do to things and what we enjoy and suffer from things in consequence. Under such conditions, doing becomes a trying; an experiment with the world to find out what it is like; the undergoing becomes an instruction—the discovery of the connection of things. (DE, 140; MW 9:147)

Reflection is provoked when a situation is indeterminate, when as it stands it is experienced as incomplete, unsettling. What readily comes to mind are those moments in the classroom when in the midst of activity, of routine, and of responding to children, we sense "something," a quality, we have a "feeling"—those moments that make us pause to scan the room and search within self. Reflection is a seeking, "a quest for something that is not at hand"—that pause in which we struggle to give form to what we sense and feel. It is in the process of inquiry, in giving serious and consecutive consideration, that an indeterminate situation is transformed into one that is "so determinate in its constituent distinctions and relations as to convert the elements of the original situation into a unified whole" (LTI, 104–105; LW 12:108–109).

Indeterminate is a general term that encompasses confusion, doubt, ambiguity, unsettlement. In the interaction between the individual and the environment, there are instances when an unsettled *quality* is *felt* or *had* by the individual. That quality belongs to the situation "just as it is." It is not general uncertainty that is sensed but a particular uncertainty, specific to and resulting from the uniqueness of the situation, of *this* interaction between organism and environment. It is this uniqueness to which the individual responds. In this sensing, pre-reflective response to the situation, there is the stirring of inquiry but not its inception.

What evokes inquiry and gives it rise is the encounter with the qualitative, the sensing and feeling of unsettlement. At this pre-reflective, pre-intentional point there is neither a problem nor inquiry. There is only the experiencing of an indeterminate situation. There is confusion because the outcome cannot be anticipated; there is conflict when "discordant responses" are evoked. Inquiry begins when the situation requires it, when awareness of the problem comes into being. That which has been directly grasped or had moves toward formulation and articulation. In this phase of the process of inquiry, the problem is located and defined. It is at this point that what is "merely an 'emotional' quality" of the whole situation is intellectualized. As when our pause and scanning in response to a felt quality in the room locates the "felt" in rising voices, increased action that seems to be motion for its own sake. We give form to the felt with words as we begin our inner conversation, "What's happening?" "Should we start snack earlier?" "Do they need refocusing?" "Who?"

Thought and Feeling

In discussing reflection and the process of inquiry, Dewey makes several points about feelings, attitudes, and emotions. Some will be presented here to balance what may seem to be a primarily intellectual undertaking. In *How We Think* Dewey describes some personal attitudes that constitute a readiness "to consider in a thoughtful way" (HWT, 28–34; LW 8:134–139). These attitudes also may be seen as predispositions, the habits of mind and heart, necessary in a democratic society. Reflection is more than knowledge about the principles of logical reasoning and skill in logical ordering. Among the attitudes described is *open-mindedness:* a willingness to entertain new ideas; "an active desire to listen to more than one side"; freedom from partisanship that closes the mind; giving full attention to alternative possibilities; recognizing the "possibility of error even in the beliefs that are dearest to us"; the cultivation "of alert curiosity and spontaneous outreaching for the new" (HWT, 30; LW 8:136). In varied ways, Dewey is characterizing active habit and plasticity, and the vitality of perception. Another attitude important to reflection is *whole-heartedness,* that is, to be thoroughly interested, with a "whole heart," in the issue at hand. Genuine enthusiasm operates as an intellectual force. Questions occur spontaneously; suggestions pour in. Matters of genuine interest hold and busy the mind (HWT, 31; LW 8:137).

As important as genuine enthusiasm and wholeheartedness may be to sustaining reflection, carrying an intellectual task to completion depends on the existence of an attitude of *intellectual responsibility.* It is such responsibility that ensures the unity essential to reflection. To be intellectually responsible requires consideration of the consequences of projected action; "intellectual responsibility secures integrity; that is to say, consistency and harmony in belief" (HWT 32; LW 8:138). The same thought is echoed in *Democracy and Education* when Dewey discusses routine and capricious behavior and finds in both a refusal "to acknowledge responsibility for the future consequences which flow from present action. Reflection is the acceptance of such responsibility" (DE, 146; MW 9:53).

It is also in *Democracy and Education* that Dewey refines the connection between thought and feeling. While observing that "reflection also implies concern with the issue," an interest in the outcome, he notes a paradox.

> From this dependence of the act of thinking upon a sense of sharing in the consequences of what goes on, flows one of the chief paradoxes of thought. Born in partiality, in order to accomplish its tasks it must achieve a certain detached impartiality. (DE, 147; MW 9:154)

It is the movement toward impartiality that characterizes the latter phases of inquiry, which "mark off a distinctive reflective experience from one on the trial and error plane" (DE, 150; MW 9:157). Returning to the earlier phases of the process of inquiry, once the problem is located and defined, the first idea that occurs, "springs up," "it pops into the mind." The intellectual element at this moment consists in what we do with the idea. The facts or data "set the problem." How the problem is conceived affects the process of inquiry and controls the ideas leading toward solution of the problem. Facts or data do not in themselves deliver solutions. Data are not given, they are selected.

Solution of a problem requires that one move beyond the immediately given of the situation to hypothesize possible connections to objects and events not present. A chain of possible connections is created linking the immediately present with absent possibilities. An interplay occurs between hypotheses and data and in shuttling between the two, viewing each within the possibilities of the other, the sense of the problem "becomes more adequate and refined" (HWT, 110; LW 8:203).

What is needed next in the process of inquiry is reasoning, the "rational elaboration" of the problem. It is here that connections are made to other information, to other meanings. These connections are then reviewed in relation to the hypotheses that have been formulated. Reasoning affects a suggested solution much as renewed observation may affect the original perception of what constituted the problem in the situation. Reasoning supplies connecting links within the situation; elements originally in seeming conflict become linked together into a consistent whole. It is this unification of disparate, conflicting elements into a comprehensible whole that is the purpose of inquiry and its definition. What remains is for the hypothesis to be tested by overt action "to give experimental corroboration, or verification of the conjectural idea" (HWT, 113–114; LW 8: 205). Through reasoning, it is hypothesized that *if* a certain plan is adopted certain consequences follow. What is needed is to determine whether ideas posed theoretically work in reality.

The description of the process of inquiry need not occur in the fixed order of presentation, and situations occur in which phases fuse or are hurried over. No set rules can be laid down since much depends on the complexity of the actual situation and the "intellectual tact and sensitiveness" of the individual. When the anticipated results of an idea do not work out as hypothesized, the situation becomes an opportunity for learning, as "failure is not *mere* failure. It is instructive" (HWT, 114; LW 8: 206). A failed experiment indicates that further observations must be made, connections reviewed, and hypotheses revised and modified.

When action does result in the realization of anticipated projections, the indeterminate, unsettled situation is transformed. It comes together; it makes sense once again. It becomes sufficiently stable in its meaning to enable the person to act and to proceed with some level of assurance and predictability. Qualifications—the insertion of words such as "some," "sufficiently"—appear because degree is the most that can be offered in terms of certainty and conclusions in a world of changing situations and possibilities. "The 'settlement' of a particular situation by a particular inquiry is no guarantee that *that* settled conclusion will always remain settled" (LTI, 8; LW 12:16). What may be attained through the process of inquiry is "warranted assertibility." With this cumbersome phrase Dewey is indicating the ongoingness of inquiry and his departure from absolutes. It is a phrase that suggests possibility rather than settlement and refers to the spatiotemporal nature of the "settled."

Dewey's approach to inquiry, and the attitudes and dispositions he outlines, are not restricted to the subjects of science or reserved for technical or lofty matters. It is an approach pertinent and applicable to the myriad problematic situations confronting us in our daily experiencing, the ever present moral dilemmas we encounter. The subject matter of inquiry is derived from the complex interactions between the person and the natural and social environment, interactions that create the situations of our daily valuing and choosing, our personal dilemmas. Not to be obscured in elucidating the process of inquiry is that what has been described is experience and living. Inquiry is a means for coping with dilemmas in a manner informed by intelligence and imagination, a creative intelligence, which enables and empowers the person in living. "Freedom is found in that kind of interaction which maintains an environment in which human desire and choice count for something. There are in truth forces in man as well as without him" (HNC, 11; MW 14:9). The conduct of life cannot (or should not) be left to chance or accident. People act and the directions they take are the result of choices they make. Consideration of the consequences of action brings with it the assumption of responsibility, which in turn surfaces questions concerning valuing and moral choice.

The appeal for Dewey of experimental inquiry, the scientific method, is obvious, for it contains so many of the characteristics he values. It is a process open to examination, to experimentation, to communication, to being shared. It demands an attitude of flexibility, openness, the absence of bias or the perpetuation of unexamined, cherished beliefs. Inquiry requires the presence of imagination in order to see new possibilities and to unearth unseen connections. It asks venturing into the unknown, accepting the risk of questioning, and concern and caring for the issue at hand. In the "experiment with the world to find out what it is like," Dewey requires the presence of imagination, openness, anticipation, and the wholeheartedness of the person. In making these qualities necessary to the experience of inquiry, he strengthens the possibility that the fulfillment, the aesthetic potential, present in all experiencing may be grasped and realized. While articulating and detailing at great length the process of inquiry, reflection, and the problematic in living, for Dewey the paradigmatic experience is the *aesthetic*–the experiencing of unity, fulfillment, and wholeness.

RELATED READINGS

Bernstein, R. (1966). *John Dewey*. New York: Washington Square Press.

Geiger, G. R. (1958). *John Dewey in perspective*. Westport, CT: Greenwood Press.

Kestenbaum, V. (1977). *The phenomenological sense of John Dewey*. Atlantic Highlands, NJ: Humanities Press.

6

Experiencing Self and World in an Early Childhood Setting

> The more definitely and sincerely it is held that education is a develop-
> ment within, by, and for experience, the more important it is that there
> shall be clear conceptions of what experience is. Unless experience is so
> conceived that the result is a plan for deciding upon subject-matter,
> upon methods of instruction and discipline, and upon material organi-
> zation of the school, it is wholly in the air.
>
> (EE, 28; LW 13:13)

To say that "education is a development within, by, and for experience" does not in itself indicate or name anything that is self-
evident. Experience and education are not simply or directly
equated to each other. The meaning of "within, by, and for" must be
made explicit if experience and education are to be connected. To accept
experience as a basis for education, for children's experiences to be used as
a source for learning, requires that a theoretical framework and criteria be
established. Dewey cautioned consistently against the mindless abandonment of the organizing, selecting, and guiding function of the teacher to a
romantic, sentimental view that sees the child's experience as supplying
both the content of curriculum as well as its direction and organization.
To do so is to place the responsibility of educating upon the child.

CRITERIA FOR EVALUATING
EDUCATIVE EXPERIENCES

An underlying assumption that serves as a foundation for connecting
experience and education is the understanding that for experience to be
educative it must lead to further growth, to further experiencing, to fuller,

enriched living. "Since growth is the characteristic of life, education is all one with growing; it has no end beyond itself" (DE, 53; MW 9:58). To break into the possible circularity of this thought, it is necessary to examine Dewey's view of growth as that which expands and enriches living. Growth is not merely an additive process of increase, nor an unfolding from within, but a qualitative movement toward a particular ideal of consummatory, conscious, intelligent living. For growth to be what Dewey intended, it must enlarge and intensify living; it must stretch horizons and swell possibilities. It must empower the social individual. Making growth an essential connecting link between experience and education is a necessary beginning, but more detail is needed in order to plan and create curriculum.

In articulating criteria for judging the educative value of experience, Dewey is guaranteeing that attention will be given in the educational setting to all the elements important to experience as a source of learning and continued growth—habit, quality, context, situation, transaction. The function the criteria serve for Dewey is to ensure that when education is based on experience, teachers will include in their thinking those elements that are essential to making experience both a means and an end in education.

It is of interest to note the time and context in which these criteria were stated. In 1938, more than two decades after the publication of his major work in education, *Democracy and Education,* Dewey once again turned his specific attention to educational practice and theory with the slim volume, *Experience and Education.* While contrasting traditional and progressive education, Dewey directed his criticism to those progressive educators who in their enthusiastic rejection of the rigidity and conformity of the philosophy and practices of traditional education had also abandoned the need for organization and philosophical grounding in their own work. In focusing their attention on what they rejected in traditional education, they neglected the need to simultaneously develop their own comprehensive frame of reference as progressive educators and risked, as Dewey observed, developing "their principles negatively rather than positively and constructively" (EE, 20; LW 13:7).

Interaction

As the transaction between organism and environment is basic to Dewey's concept of experience, he ensures its inclusion in our thinking by stating that a

> chief principle for interpreting an experience in its educational function and force [assigns] equal rights to both factors in experience—objective and inter-

nal conditions. Any normal experience is an interplay of these two sets of
conditions. Taken together, or in their interaction, they form what we call a
situation. (EE, 42; LW 13:24)

Dewey is stressing that if experience is to be a source for learning-growth,
equal attention must be given to the child and the environment. It is the
interaction of the two that creates the situation; the qualities to which the
child responds are in the situation. Dewey does not want to tip the scale in
either direction. In traditional education, the balance was tipped to favor
the importance of objective conditions and thereby lessened or inhibited
children's possibilities to construct their knowledge or to achieve personal
meanings. In the "planless improvisations" of some progressive educators,
greater weight was given to the immediately pleasurable world of the child
without attending to expanding connections or extending possibilities.
Dewey is striving for neither the subjective nor objective to be subordinate
to the other in the teacher's planning.

Assigning "equal rights to both factors in experience" signifies that in
terms of the subjective it is our task to know as fully as possible the
children with whom we work: to understand their attitudes and predispositions; to acknowledge the experiences they have had and the connections
they have made; to seek what awakens their curiosity and the meanings
they have created; to know and respect their story. Growing out of our
understanding of the child, we are asked to create an environment in
which children may find and make significant, meaningful connections to
their own lives and that also will elicit and release potential and imagination. The classroom environments we create will acknowledge time by
responding to the continuum of a child's experiencing. They will connect
the child's familiar, remembered past with an alive, developing present.
And further, the environment will generate an invitation to enter an unknown future of risk, possibility, and surprise with willingness and anticipation.

The unstructured and open-ended materials and activities explored in
Chapter 3 are means well-suited for young children to experience their
world, to pose their questions, to express and refine the meanings they
have given to self and world. Materials such as clay, paint, water, blocks,
wood, crayons, and paper and activities such as cooking, planting, trips,
movement, sewing, and weaving offer children direct, sensorial, manipulative opportunities for experiencing the texture of the world in which they
live. As children interact with materials and participate in classroom activities, the world enters through the senses. Touching, tasting, hearing,
seeing, smelling–the world is taken in. It is in such experiencing that a
selected, interpreted base is created from which children begin to form

expectations, make connections, and enter the organized knowledge of the world. In the selected, arranged environment of the classroom, the knowledge and activities of the world, often remote and mysterious for the young, come within the reach of the child. In giving children ample time and space for exploration, and materials as means, the larger world is made accessible and manageable, slowed down sufficiently so that it may be held and probed in a variety of ways and personally understood.

Continuity

What has been said about interaction and the consideration given to time, leads to the second criterion stated by Dewey. For experience to be educative, there also must be continuity. "The principle of continuity of experience means that every experience both takes up something from those which have gone before and modifies in some way the quality of those which come after" (EE, 35; LW 13:19). Continuity exists when "experience is a moving force," when it arouses "curiosity, strengthens initiative and sets up desires and purposes" (EE, 38; LW 13:21–22). The two principles–continuity and interaction–are not separate from each other.

> They intercept and unite. They are, so to speak, the longitudinal and lateral aspects of experience. Different situations succeed one another. But because of the principle of continuity something is carried over from the earlier to the later ones. As an individual passes from one situation to another, his world, his environment, expands or contracts. He does not find himself living in another world but in a different part or aspect of one and the same world. What he has learned in the way of knowledge and skill in one situation becomes an instrument of understanding and dealing effectively with the situations which follow. The process goes on as long as life and learning continue. (EE, 44; LW 13:25–26)

In emphasizing the principle of continuity, Dewey is calling attention to plasticity and habit: the person's attitudes and predispositions; the prior meanings by which the world is encountered; the adaptive actions and means constructed by the person in interaction with the environment. Habits that remain plastic and open to encounter are the threads of continuity that enable the person to "take up something, from those [experiences] which have gone before" and that modify in some way "the quality of those which come after" (EE, 35; LW 13:19). Emphasizing continuity in the interaction between the subjective and objective, Dewey is asking us to actively remember the nature of the person. The subjective of which he speaks is a particular subject–a person of active habits and potential, selec-

tively seeking meaning and significance in interaction with the environment. And the environment is "whatever conditions interact with personal
needs, desires, purposes, and capacities to create the experience which is
had" (EE, 44; LW 13:25).

IMPLICATIONS FOR CURRICULUM PLANNING
AND TEACHING

The two criteria for evaluating the educative worth of an experience–
continuity and interaction–underline the necessity of including the active
participation of children in curriculum planning for it is *their* experience
that is under consideration: their individual experiencing and their experiences as a group. And here it is helpful to remember the distinction between recognition and perception, which would caution us to leave room
in our thinking for a child's uniqueness, the individuality that departs in
some way from theoretical descriptions and formulations. What we make
of a child's experience is not synonymous with the experience of the child,
which is what it is–a qualitative occurrence in a situation. We may come
closer to understanding children's experience by offering them the means
by which to express what has been experienced, and by providing opportunities for them to examine, connect, and transform their experience.

The criteria also ask us to think about our part in the child's experience. And here we must be careful not to commit what I would call the
"educational fallacy." It is not a phrase to be found in Dewey's writings but
grows out of applying his thought to classroom practice. The "educational
fallacy" would be to confuse the *offering* of an *opportunity* to experience as
being the *giving* of an experience. This seemingly small distinction carries
with it far-reaching implications for teachers and children. We may be
part of a child's experience, we may influence a child's experience, but an
experience cannot be given. Experiences are had, not *given*. The most we
can offer is the *opportunity* to experience through the social and physical
environment we create. To think otherwise is to negate all that has been
said about interaction, situation, quality, habit, the selecting, interpreting
nature of the person, and, in a most basic sense, denies the power of the
child. If experience is given, once again, the child becomes a receptacle to
be filled, an enactor of the intentions and purposes of others.

In the educational implications derived from the concept of the social
individual, attention was given primarily to the type of social and physical
environments that would support the growth of the child's potential and
capacity and of community and communication. Observations and choices
in curricular matters were guided by Dewey's view of the nature of the

person. Although this concern remains central in thinking and planning, it now becomes the context in which present remarks and choices are grounded. The nature of the person–the social individual–is now assumed. The person remains "constant" while a shift occurs in the kinds of questions we ask. What effect does the variety in experience have on our curriculum planning? Are there additional factors to be considered in relation to what has been said about materials, activities, time, space, and the social and physical environment when the focus is on the experiencing of the social individual?

With experience as our vantage point, when planning the objective conditions of the classroom, our thinking now includes consideration of unspoken qualities. The classroom is understood not only as an environment (a general place) but also as myriad situations in which personal meanings and connections emerge (personal places particularized by time and quality). Attending to experience, the choices we have made about space, materials, activities require review. How may the environment I have created be sensed by the child? What are its unspoken messages? Asking such questions is a vantage point for revealing the multiple "isms" of exclusion that permeate our classrooms and society. What attention have I given to the continuity of experience? In the selections and arrangements I have made is one type of experiencing given primacy? Does the environment genuinely acknowledge that children come with experiences, with habits, with prior meanings–that neither the children nor the classroom exists in isolation, out of context? What invitations are offered?

The description of a morning visit to a kindergarten classroom in late spring may concretize what has been said about quality and illustrate the influence and effect of the social atmosphere on learning and the emergence or suppression of self and interest.

Along with the day's usual activities of painting, drawing, math, manipulatives, block building, and writing, two special events were scheduled. First, five first graders were invited to come speak to the kindergarten children about life in first grade, and later that morning the kindergarten children would visit a first-grade classroom. In preparation for these events, the children joined in discussion to prepare their questions, which their teacher Barbara wrote on a chart. The first question was, "Do you have gym in first grade?" followed by, "Do you play in first grade?" And last, "Do you have homework?"

The first graders arrived and sat on the floor facing the younger children. Barbara told them that the group had some questions and read the first one. The first graders turned their attention to the teacher and began speaking to her. She moved further away and directed the visitors' attention to the eager kindergarten group.

Questions were asked. Yes, first grade did include gym and there was time to play. To make sure, one of the children asked, "When do you have it?" "In the afternoon." Then, the big question about homework and the more specific, "Is it hard?" The responses were mixed: three "No, it isn't"; one "Yes, a little"; and one "Yeah, sometimes." At this point the teacher of the first grade came into the room and added, "We don't start homework until January." There was great relief among the younger children and the awakening of memories among the older ones—"Oh, yeah! That's right!" "Right! Not at the beginning. I forgot that." And finally, the basic question was asked, "Did you know to read?" Again, there were varied responses and among them the reassuring "It's O.K. Don't worry. They'll teach you." As the first graders left, the kindergartners talked animatedly among themselves. Jackson said, "I know all about first grade. My brother was in it." Maria said to her friend, "See, *I told you,* they play."

Later that morning, the kindergartners visited a first-grade classroom. As they entered the room, the quickly moving children slowed down. They looked around the room at all the signs and printed words, at the order of the shelves filled with math materials, and at the individual desks that replaced their familiar tables. They sat on the floor facing the first graders and their teacher, who sat on a chair next to her class. The teacher welcomed the children and began telling them of life in first grade—the rules, the hard work, the homework, and more rules. The participation of the first graders consisted of giving the details of the rules, of describing a ritual called "desk check," and of making observations such as, "In first grade when a teacher says, 'I'd like you to . . . ' that means you have to." Throughout these comments and explanations, the visiting children sat silently. There were no questions; there was no movement. When they left, they looked straight ahead and walked quickly.

Earlier that morning, it was not only the comfort and security of being in their own room that helped the children to voice personal concerns, to make connections, and to ask hard questions. Essential to the atmosphere of the room was the teacher's movement away from center stage to the background. Barbara gave the occasion to the children and in doing so she strengthened their voices. Her movement gave permission to the first graders to be teachers, and for the kindergartners it was an honoring of the worth and importance of their questions and comments. In and through their discussion, the children gave form to their anxieties; in conversation with others they discovered they were not alone in their fears; sharing their thoughts and feelings, they reassured each other. Those who were too hesitant to speak, heard their concerns voiced by others. It was *their* meeting even though Barbara did not withdraw completely. She observed and listened carefully. She prompted when needed, "Didn't you have a question to ask?" To another child who had difficulty forming a question, she asked, "What do you think about that?" And there was reassurance also in hearing the varied responses of the visiting first graders—homework could be easy; it could be a little hard; and, yes, sometimes it was hard. It's easier to find one's place along a continuum of possibilities.

In the visit to the first grade, the teacher also set the tone. She imparted information; she spoke of rules. The first graders confirmed the future she described as did the labeled order of the classroom. And although the teacher cheerfully asked, "Are there any questions?" none surfaced. There were no pauses, no space, either in her presentation or in the filled organization of the room, that genuinely invited the expression of the children's concerns or interests, or indicated that there would be room for their play and questions. They took their questions, and feelings, with them as they left the room. In each instance the quality in the situation determined the kind of experiences the children had—in one there was expansion and anticipation and in the other silence and withdrawal.

Acknowledgment of the significance of quality influences and broadens our perspective. Responding to quality means that we do not focus merely on behavior or on specific tasks or activities. Attention must be extended to include understanding that the activity of the child is part of a situation. It is to understand that acting, behaving, doing are located within a context and that context is qualitative. It is endowed with particular meaning by the individual, meaning achieved by the person. To look merely at a child's performance or skills in reading is insufficient; attending to quality, it is necessary to view qualitatively and to consider the child's experience of reading. The act of reading, the mastery of skills, then are viewed within a context, a framework of meaning, and in relation to the contribution each makes to the total functioning of the person. Skills should not become isolated badges of accomplishment. They must be related to what they contribute to the total functioning of the person, to how they affect what exists, to what use they may be put by the person in interaction with the environment. Such a perspective or attitude insists upon integration, both in connection with a whole self and further to the interrelationship among skills, for they also must be viewed holistically.

In addressing the qualitative, what was said in a previous chapter about teachers being fully present in their teaching is now re-emphasized. To be fully present, consciously aware, is to be open to nuance, to the sense and feel of the immediate, to that which is not readily apparent and often left unspoken. Attention to experience and the qualitative also underlines the statements made about anticipation and ongoingness as part of the teacher's attitude, for both are affairs of time—time in which to be sensed, to stretch and infer, to become complete. What is also underscored is the uniqueness of each child and the particularity of situations, and the consistent attention to be given to potentiality and possibility.

These observations about quality are derived from a broad view of experience. Discussion becomes more particular when we look at the variety in experiencing. Beginning with pre-reflective experience, what is pertinent for us as teachers arises not so much in terms of direct application to classroom practice but as a guide to that which is to be avoided. The child's response to the qualitative in a situation determines the path experiencing will take, what it will become. Characteristic of experiences that do not become a "moving force" are those in which the person's response is one of fragmentation, withdrawal, distraction, and inattention. The quality in a situation is disrupted by mechanical responses and "seeing without feeling." Perception is arrested when touch and contact remain tangential, when context is minimized or neglected by abstracting and focusing on one element of a situation. Each of these responses short-circuits the possibilities of the further development of an experience. Any of these responses limits the "might be" of living, the coming into existence of new situations and responses.

Looked at closely, the itemizing of "disrupters" of experience may also be seen as a listing of what happens daily in many classrooms. It is more than unfortunate that in those environments that are specifically arranged to promote learning and growth, it is these disrupters of experiencing that often seem to prevail. The observations of classroom researchers such as Jackson (1968), Goodlad (1984; Goodlad, Klein, & Associates, 1970), Lortie (1975) and others are replete with examples of teaching that directs children to stereotypic, mundane, mechanical responses, to fragmented acts of seeing and contacting, to teacher-directed activities focusing on isolated aspects of situations and events. The imperative and omnipresent "look" and "see" of adults tend to close eyes and create tunnel vision rather than serve the function of awakening perception and illuminating perspective. Too often, children are asked to "merely recognize," to stop short where they are and to fix the world into given knowns, rather than being asked to actively perceive and to make new connections and to reconstruct experience. In contrast to the sterile "look" and "see," "what do you see?" is an opening for the child's contribution, an opportunity for the child to select, interpret, and give form to an event. The latter approach also creates an opening for the teacher to see into the child's world, to learn how the child grasps the world in which they both live. Honest questions serving as true communication between people are an eliciting endeavor wherein adults and children share perceptions and amend and enlarge each other's view. A question is honest when the asker is truly interested in the response of the other, when the dialogue initiated is not *pro forma*.

A question frequently asked of children is, "Are you finished?" Sometimes, that question is asked as an indirect prompt to children to finish what they are doing. In the situation to be described, the question was asked genuinely and the manner in which it was posed, through words and action, honored the child's world. It is midmorning in a class of four- and five-year-olds who are busy in various activities throughout the room. The art teacher in the school has come to the room to work with a small group of children. Three tray set-ups for painting have been placed on tables and each child has been given the three primary colors and white and black. Then the teacher, Lois, added turquoise blue to each tray.

LOIS: I'm giving you a little turquoise blue.
CHILD: Why a little?
LOIS: When it's a little you have to think about it.
CHILD: A little can be a lot.
LOIS: That's how artists think.

Uninvolved in this exchange was four-year-old Mitch, who was busily mixing many colors and energetically placing dabs of the colors in different directions. At one point he announced, "I'm finished." Lois knelt and commented on the various colors, their placement, and the movement in Mitch's painting. She then held up the painting and asked, "Are you finished?" Mitch scanned the painting slowly and carefully and said, "No." Lois placed the paper on the table. Mitch dipped his brush in three colors and with great concentration, bending over the paper, he placed large dabs of the mixed color on the top right-hand corner of his painting. He looked at his painting and said, "Finished." Lois held it up again and asked, "Are you finished?" Without hesitation, he nodded his head and said, "Yes." Carefully, he lifted the painting from the middle of the sides of the paper so that no paint would drip and took it out to the hall to dry. As he did so, his face and body reflected a sense of accomplishment, of satisfaction and completion. Lois's honestly asked, "Are you finished?" combined with the offering of a different perspective of his painting–by holding it up and thus offering him another vantage point from which to view his painting– gave Mitch an opportunity to experience his work, to see it freshly, and to make choices.

Many incidents that may limit experience occur because of the distinction Dewey makes between perception and mere recognition, when perception is "arrested at the point where it will serve some other purpose." These are the times when teachers narrowly direct perception toward a didactic end while overlooking children's experimental, "messing about" style of making connections, their lingering and savoring approach to life. Prompted, and often rushed, by stated goals of curriculum outlines, there are times when we settle for a facade of language–imitated words that create an appearance of learning–but actually hide a shaky foundation of delivered connections made by others.

Along with the limitations that may occur because of the mismatch between process-oriented searching and product-oriented teaching, there are other ways in which experiences may be arrested. A great disrupter to children's experiencing is how time is conceived by adults. What may be added here is that as we think about time–as flow or measure, as something possessed or possessing–we are offered an opportunity to confront whether we genuinely accept and believe that children do learn from experience, and that education is a development "within, by, and for experience." It becomes difficult to include in the curriculum the stretches of time needed for experiences to flow, extend, become complete, if we do not believe that children's own questions are significant and worthwhile and that their observations and comments are pertinent to inquiry. Only then will time be created within the schedule for children to pursue their connections and meanings. The "having of wonderful ideas" does not just happen.

> There are two aspects to providing occasions for wonderful ideas. One is being willing to accept children's ideas. The other is providing a setting that suggests wonderful ideas to children–different ideas to different children–as they are caught up in intellectual problems that are real to them. (Duckworth, 1987, p. 7)

We may find evidence in research studies to support this view of experiential learning, of personal constructing and inventing, of the social context of learning. Yet, within this perspective there also exists a "leap of faith"–faith in the continuum of experience, in intrinsic motivation, in the belief that personally rooted searching can lead and connect to objectively organized knowing. At the same time, that leap does not cancel our sensitive and informed participation in the educational undertaking. There are questions to be asked, materials to be provided, activities to be planned, interactions to be facilitated, possibilities to be expanded. A "leap of faith" does not mean that we stand by passively awaiting experience to do its work.

EXPERIENCE AND PLAY

The role of play in human development has held the interest of writers in many fields. Theories abound as the topic is viewed from varied perspectives. Although millions of words have been written about play, it remains essentially unlimited by definition. The difficulties attending the definition of play are multiple and complex. Like breathing and walking, play is something that children do. Children are the initiators, creators, inventors, maintainers, and "doers" of play. It is theirs. Play is a qualitative affair. We have entered a domain where qualities are grasped in their immediacy, where in the activity of the child "each successive part flows freely," where action has its own "rhythm that carries." With play we are often in the presence of aesthetic experiencing. Words and imposed structures only approximate the richness and fullness of such experiences rather than define them.

The play activities of children vary in form, function, and meaning. Play has been characterized as "imitative," "cathartic," "assimilatory," "pretend," "imaginative." Labels and categories multiply as the activity is observed from different vantage points. In early childhood, play is used by teachers as a label in a variety of ways, reflecting differing perspectives and understanding of the activity. The word may be used to distinguish between teacher-directed and child-initiated activities (the former being work, the latter play); refer to the activities of an area (house play, outdoor play, water play); describe activity that by the adult's standards does not seem goal-directed or purposeful ("they're just playing with those shapes"); describe a child's or children's activity that seems to have some element of narrative within it that has been initiated by the participant(s) (commonly referred to as dramatic play); refer to the social make-up of the activity or to a developmental stage (solitary, parallel, cooperative, group play).

The stated or implied polarization of work and play is a distinction that has been made about human activities over the centuries, another example of the either/or constructs that limit choice and possibilities. For children, work and play become separate categories as adults differentiate and name their activities. Our task as teachers is to understand this powerful and dominant mode of children and to utilize it to a significant degree in curriculum planning. Few activities can so fully address the principles that connect experience and education as does play. This statement is not restricted to the lower range of early childhood. It is significant throughtout the continuum and sorely missed in school settings by children in primary grades. While the form of play changes with age, the spirit of play—experimentation, imagination, freedom, transformation—remains.

As children interact with the environment, as they encounter situations and events, they select information, raise questions, put "things together," and try to make sense of it all. Habits, ways of grasping and holding on to the world, are formed. Feelings and thoughts are sorted and organized, meanings achieved. One of the most profound means available to children for constructing and reconstructing experience, formulating and reformulating their experience is through play. Play is a means for synthesis and integration in that it brings together the child's concept of reality with the inner world of feelings and imaginings. In play children create hypotheses and meander among ideas and experiences, and while playing they reveal their questions, their ambivalences, their fears and hopes, their wishes and conflicts. Questions that are sensed rather than formed find expression and formulation in play. It is in children's dramatic play that we can see the variety in experience that Dewey discusses – pre-reflective, aesthetic, and inquiry/problem solving – as children transform their experience by adding, embellishing, imagining, changing, shifting, transforming, condensing, and expanding what has been and what might be. There are interesting parallels to be found between the variety in experience that Dewey describes and the development of children's use of materials. In the section that follows, one material, blocks, is used to explore the concept of experience in relation to the development of children's use of materials. The development described in children's use of blocks will be seen also in observing children use other materials such as clay, paint, and crayons. For example, there also are stages in painting – from experimentation with the liquid nature of paint applied to paper with a brush, to using intentionally the mastery one has achieved of the medium by mixing colors and making designs and patterns, to the representational forms that fuse thought and feeling. Each material offers children another opportunity and means with which they can tell their emerging stories about self and world.

PLAY, MATERIALS, AND EXPERIENCE

As an unstructured, open-ended material, blocks offer multiple opportunities to children. They may be used primarily to discover their structural possibilities. They may be used aesthetically as in the creation of forms and for the translation of architectural ideas. Blocks may also be used to express the child's increasing understanding of self and world, as when the structures they build combine with dramatic/narrative content and children construct and function within symbolic worlds of farms, airports, supermarkets, police stations, houses, and space stations, as did the children in the extended anecdote about traffic. In the years of early childhood a progression appears in the use of blocks. It is within this continuum of development that parallels may be found to pre-reflective, aesthetic, and inquiry-focused experiencing.

The initial response of young children to a material is basically exploratory, an attempt to find out "what can I do with this?" As purpose is not necessarily involved in the child's activity, "what does this do" may more accurately reflect the young child's attitude. As children stack blocks, stand them on end, watch them topple, push them across the floor, or set one atop the other in a bridging pattern, they are involved in open-ended experimentation. It is in such trial and error doing, such seemingly aimless (to the adult) explorations that the properties of a material are discovered and possibilities investigated. Over time and with repeated use, the child comes to know that blocks do not bend or break. Blocks fall. They have different shapes and they are smooth. It is in the exploratory, trial and error approach of the young child that some similarity may be found to pre-reflective experiencing. It is an approach to be honored for it is in such "messing about" that discoveries may be made and insights informed. It is a time needed by children to create their own base of understanding from which to venture into the unknown. As the child experiences a material, an interaction regulated by the tempo and interests of the child, possibilities are born and qualities grasped. Directing activity toward representation during this exploratory stage limits the child's possibilities. The message, the collateral learning, in such premature structuring of experimentation is a diminishing of the child's budding perception of self as a source of power and ability.

Within this experimental process one may also find instances that manifest kinship to aesthetic experiencing, as when the activity of the child takes on a quality of wholeness and completion, those moments when self and material fuse and together become the essence of a thing or situation. There are moments, sometimes fleeting, when a young child moves a block along the floor, lifts it abruptly, whirs with swaying, lilting motions of the body across the room. Immediate time and space are transcended. The child and block become one, a unity expressing the essence of *helicopterness*. It is an instance of wholeness where "every successive part flows freely, without seam and without unfilled blanks, into what ensues" (AE, 36; LW 10:43).

As the child gains mastery over the physical properties of a material, when one comes to know what to expect from blocks, attention turns to creating forms. In this phase of block building, the structures created by the child are often like sculpture, for function and representation are not primary concerns. For the child, the structure often is an unlabeled expression. It simply *is*. The child's attention is given to creating an object in space, a form that satisfies, an expression of relationships among planes and angles, openings and closures. The child's attitude toward such building is clearly evident in the fact that these structures often are not used by the child upon completion. What remains behind, as the child walks away, may be a structure of exceptional beauty, of daring, breathtaking balancing and subtle patterns of light and surfaces. It can be difficult at such times to accept the child's "abandonment" of his or her structure, or to silence the curiosity that evokes the intruding "What is it?", a question of little concern to the child.

Certain distinctions are necessary. To be aware that the response of the adult to a child's efforts may influence the child's experience and its meaning to the child, does not necessarily mean that the adult is to remain a mute, passive observer. The challenge for the teacher is to respond in a manner *compatible* to the nature of the child's experiencing and to join the child in his or her present. This may require a shift in mind-set. It is not always necessary for us to point to, to label, to categorize, to make known, to analyze. There are, as Dewey said, "poetic and moral meanings." If we want children to grasp and become sensitive to the poetic, the aesthetic, the moral in life (while not even knowing that categories of meaning exist), then we are asked to think about what response would match and honor the child's vision—as in Lois's respectful and sensitive response to Mitch's painting and to the questions of the other children.

While experimental trials and aesthetic expression remain, with time the child also moves in the direction of intentional building. Here, children approach blocks with a purpose in mind, an intention born of the moment or planned ahead. An example of such play was the story of the children who dealt with the traffic problems that occurred around their structures—the hospital, the pizza store, the police station, homes, and the castle. The interactions that emerged in play as the children functioned in a social world they had created were examined in relation to the social individual. The play could have been viewed also from the vantage point of the children's experience in the dramas they created.

Play and Education

While accepting Dewey's criteria that connect experience and education and his view of education as a social process, questions still remain when thinking of play as a source for learning and curriculum development. Is children's play pertinent primarily for observation of their interests and development? Are there entry points for teachers in children's play? Do we introduce themes into children's play? Or do we guide/shape play primarily through questions, discussions, and trips? Is there a difference between these two approaches? How is the partnership in curriculum development realized when play is central? How do we approach play in order to realize the potential of the social individual, develop a sense of community, and surface individual questions and interests?

One way to consider these questions is to think about space and materials in relation to an area found commonly in classrooms of three-, four-, and five-year-olds and identified by a variety of names. Usually, these areas for play have articles of adult clothing for dress up, and child-sized furniture such as a stove, sink, bed, table, and chairs. The setting is varied at times by introducing items and furnishings that shift the focus of play by providing supplementary materials that suggest a doctor's office, a restaurant, a supermarket, a beach. Another way to offer children the opportunity to enact their stories and dramas is to supply fabric in a variety of textures, size, and color for dress up and to provide hollow blocks with which children construct the setting for their play. While both settings are opportunities for dramatic play, opportunities for children to question, remember, and transform their experiences in the social and physical world through their play, the former is a found setting determined by others. The latter is like a stage on which the child or children imagine the setting, and from their experiences and imagination fashion their outfits and create their version of a doctor's office, a restaurant, or supermarket.

Other examples and questions: Do we provide children with pre-mixed green, orange, and purple, or do we offer primary colors and black and white with which children create their own shades and colors? In the block area, do we purchase small furniture, offered in catalogues, for children to place in their buildings, or do children construct their own furniture with blocks or at the workbench? Do we buy the set of traffic signs or do children make their own? Do we brainstorm the multiple possibilities to be found in a theme/topic and create activities for children to explore that theme/topic in depth? Or, do we observe children's play and take from it the themes/topics to be elaborated and expanded within the context they have created?

The questions posed in this examination of children's play are a continuation of an earlier discussion on structured and unstructured materials. The posing of these juxtapositions, culled from many hours spent in classrooms, is not to create more either/ors with which to contend but rather to underline that when we connect experience and education, then it is necessary to think in detail about the consequences of our choices in relation to the environments we create, the material/texts we offer, and the kind of "moving force" they may become in children's experiencing. To be a moving force requires that there be continuity in experience, that connections exist between the child's interests and questions and the work at hand. To seek and utilize what children bring is more complex than selecting a theme/topic to introduce to children. One of the difficulties lies in having sufficient knowledge in a variety of areas so that one may successfully ask the questions that push children to probe further and deeper. Rather than experienced as problematic, these situations may also be seen as opportunities to search and learn together, revealing to children the excitement and ongoingness of learning. Possibly, a more basic complexity is sharing the control of curriculum content. In this partnership between children and teacher how we accommodate each other's interests and purposes is an ever present question and requires revisiting questions raised earlier about the selection of knowledge.

There, in presenting criteria for curriculum development, social studies was identified as an approach that gave primacy to the growth of the social individual and to understanding the complex world in which we live. The centrality of the *social* in social studies repeatedly brings questions and ideas back to people. The story and history of people's lives—their accomplishments, aspirations, struggles, hopes, and disappointments—are viewed from the perspective of different fields of knowledge. In the partnership between children's interests and questions and teachers' aims and questions, selections are made. Explicitly and implicitly, our choices contribute to the child's view of the world and his or her place in it. What children's interests shall become, what connections they make, what meanings emerge depend greatly on our responses. To which questions do we choose to give our attention? Does the social atmosphere we create invite all stories to be told? And, in addition to what children bring, what knowledge of the world, which complexities, do *we* choose to bring into the classroom? These questions will be discussed further in Chapter 8.

RELATED READINGS

Biber, B. (1959). Premature structuring as a deterrent to creativity. *American Journal of Orthopsychiatry, 1959, 24*(2), 280–290.

Biber, B. (1934). Children's drawings: From lines to pictures. *69 Bank Street Publications*. New York: Bank Street College of Education.

Eisner, E. (1990). The role of art and play in children's cognitive development. In E. Klugman, & S. Smilansky (Eds.), *Children's play and learning: Perspectives and policy implications*. New York: Teachers College Press.

Hirsch, E. S. (Ed.). (1984). *The block book* (rev. ed.). Washington, DC: National Association for the Education of Young Children.

Millar, S. (1968). *The psychology of play*. London: Pelican.

Smith, N. R., with Fucigna, C., Kennedy, M., & Lord, L. (1993). *Experience and art: Teaching children to paint* (2nd ed.). New York: Teachers College Press.

Wirth, A. G. (1966). *John Dewey as educator: His design for work in education (1894–1904)*. New York: John Wiley.

7

The Drama of Island Life

No one has ever watched a child intent in his play without being made
aware of the complete merging of playfulness and seriousness.

(AE, 279; LW 10:284)

In the extended anecdote of this chapter, the dramatic play of a kindergarten group will be viewed with a focus on experience – the aesthetic,
the pre-reflective, and instances of problem solving and the emergence
of new ideas. The anecdote also serves as an illustration of social studies
rooted in children's play; that is, an example of children learning about the
social and physical world through the dramas they create, the problems
they pose, and their search for information that helps them to make sense
of the world in which they live. In contrast to the anecdote about roads
and traffic, in this instance it is the teacher who has initiated the context of
the play.

THE BIRTH OF A HURRICANE

The setting is a kindergarten in midyear. The children's block work
had become repetitive. Dramatic play seemed random and without real
investment. Obviously something was needed to revitalize interest and to
spark new ideas. At the discussion time before work in the room began,
the teacher noted the repetitiveness of buildings and that "people don't
really seem to be interested in what they are doing." She asked the children
to think of something "you haven't done before." Work in this area had
one rule, established earlier in the year: No super heroes or any of the
current action figures.

Over the year, as the children worked in the block area, several for-
mats had evolved. From simply building initially without considering a

context into which the buildings would fit, the group had been guided into thinking about a context into which buildings were situated. For example, at one point the teacher suggested that half the floor space would be "city" and the other half "country," which then required thinking about where particular buildings would be placed. At other times, a river (two painted blue lines) ran across the floor and required thinking about bridges, boats, and highways. Changes in the environment gave rise to different structures, content, problems, and interactions and served the social studies content of the group. Each new situation created opportunities for small and whole group trips, discussions, books, and many related activities.

First Day

TEACHER: I've been thinking—what would it be like if all the floor in the block area became a river?

YVONNE: So what do we do, swim all the time?

RICHARD: You could fish, too.

YVONNE: I don't want to fish. I want to make a school.

RICHARD: You could do that.

YVONNE: (incredulous) In the river?

TODD: Wait, Wait!! I have an idea! An ocean, an ocean, all the floor an ocean.

Todd's enthusiasm is contagious and the group becomes animated but it is also evident that many children, like Yvonne, literally need grounding.

TEACHER: What about islands?

TODD: Yeah, islands!! There are islands in the ocean. That's land and you can walk on it.

Great excitement. "Islands, islands." "We'll make an island together." "Islands, hurrah!" The teacher asks, "Where will the islands be?" The response is a chorus of "in the ocean!" The teacher's question was aimed at discussing placement of the islands on the floor. Obviously the topic was too abstract to be handled only with words, so the teacher suggests, "Let's go over to the block area and figure this out. We'll see where the islands will be." Discussion starts on shape and size. Are all islands the same size? How close should the islands be to each other? How big could the biggest one be? As each person decided on island size and walked away to the block shelves to get blocks, islands were "lost." Coming back with blocks, the children were confused. "Where's my island?" "Where did my island go?" Chalk lines were made outlining each island. In that way children were free to walk away to get blocks without their islands disappearing.

For some children the chalk lines provided security but not clarity. They built in the ocean near the chalk lines or stood looking at them in perplexity. Resolution was achieved in a mixture of trying, looking at others (especially Todd, who worked without a pause), standing back and looking at the lines. Some children worked alone, others with a partner. The entire work period was taken up with constructing boundaries and buildings. On the islands in the ocean a school, an airport, a fish store, a hospital, and several homes were built. The islands were populated by small wooden and rubber figures manipulated by the children. Some children worked with one figure (the fish store) or with several figures (families with children in some homes, plus other variations such as doctors and nurses at the hospital, or, as in Yvonne's school, her teacher worked with most of the children from the various families). Some of the children began to work on details for their buildings. Steven made colorful, monster-like fish for his store with paper and crayons which he then cut out. Amy made blankets from material and drew and cut out "medicines to make people better" for her hospital.

Second Day

As the children came into the room many rushed to the block area to look at the islands. In this second day of work some of the children put their small people into the ocean pretending that they were swimming from island to island. Some of the children began to draw fish to place in the ocean along with pieces of shredded material and pieces of string to represent seaweed. (Some of this activity was sparked by a book on ocean life, which was in the class library.) Some of the incidents during the dramatic play that morning included

- A swimmer was taken to the hospital because he "bumped into a whale."
- Yvonne's schoolteacher gave swimming lessons to the schoolchildren for a while. She then announced, "It's rest time." Once the children were settled, the teacher went off to swim alone among the fish and seaweed.
- Steven sat alone at his fish store glumly awaiting customers. No one came. He was particularly annoyed with Todd, who had made a fishing pole out of a stick and string and was fishing from his airport island. Other children picked up the idea.

Third Day

The following discussion took place before the children began working in the block area.

STEVEN: It's not fair. I don't have any customers. No one buys my fish.
          Everybody is catching their own fish.
YVONNE: We don't need your store. We have the ocean. The fish are
          right there.
STEVEN: But I have the fish store.
YVONNE: But nobody NEEDS it!!

With this basic exchange on economics, Steven announced, "I'm going to
build a weather station."

TEACHER: Fine. I think that will be very helpful to the people on the
          islands.
STEVEN: And everybody has to have a radio so they can hear the
          weather. Maybe there'll be big waves.
AMY: Can children really swim in a big ocean?
TODD: If they know how to swim.
AMY: But, you know, can they swim from the island to the other
          island? Can they swim anywhere?
          [Silence.]
TODD: They could use boats. Like Jeff.

Jeff had made a small sailboat at the workbench. He sailed along paying
little attention to the activity around him, occasionally muttering, "Seaweed, lots of seaweed."

BILL: We could have a boat that goes to all the islands.
TEACHER: Do you mean a ferry?
BILL: It'll be bigger than Jeff's and a lot of people could get on it. I'll
          do it.

The inclusion of the ferry caused chaos. Bill encountered the wrath of
many irate commuters, especially when he sailed off at whim to pick up his
special friends. Yvonne, an impatient person in or out of dramatic play,
finally threw all the schoolchildren into the ocean with the terse announcement, "Swim home!"

Fourth Day

The work period began with a meeting to discuss the ferry service. Many complaints were waiting to be aired.

TEACHER: There certainly are a lot of complaints! What can we do?
TODD: Bill *has* to stop at ALL the islands.
AMY: I get tired to waiting. I don't know when he's coming. I just wait, and wait, and wait.
YVONNE: I'm making my own boat.
TEACHER: Hold on, Yvonne. Let's see if we can work this out. If everybody makes their own boat then Bill won't have a job. Remember Steven's fish store? What happened when everyone did their own fishing? Let's think about this. Is there anything that we can do?
AMY: (to Bill) Why don't you tell us when you're coming? So we don't be waiting.
BILL: You mean yell to you, "I'm coming!"
TODD: I know! Let's make a schedule like real ferries have.
BILL: What?
TODD: You see, there's a sign and it says—"the ferry's coming at ten" and then it says "the ferry is coming at eleven." And you know to be there.
BILL: I don't know the clock.
               [Silence.]
TEACHER: A lot of people don't know how to tell time yet.

The teacher initiates discussion of the meaning of a schedule. Comparisons are made with the classroom schedule, particularly to parts of the schedule that are fixed. What is finally arrived at, with considerable participation on the part of the teacher, is a fixed order of travel for the ferry. A list of that order is made into a chart and posted. Those at the beginning of the list greet the plan enthusiastically. Almost unnoticed during the remaining work period are periodic weather bulletins issued by Steven. "The sun's going away." "Very cloudy now." "May rain tomorrow." The last bulletin issued near the end of the work period—"I think there is a storm coming up"—visibly catches the attention of some children.

Fifth Day

It is Friday and the children know that before the end of the day all the blocks will be picked up. As children go about their activities in the area, fishing, swimming, attending to patients and schoolchildren, taking plane rides from the airport, Steven begins to issue storm warnings. The first is, "A very big storm is coming up." A bit later, "We think it's a hurricane. A BIG one!!" More children begin attending to the warnings, including those who are not working in the area. Two children making a design with parquetry blocks leave it on the table and walk over to the ocean. Steven's warnings come more rapidly and with greater urgency. "Yessir!! It really is a hurricane. You better go home. There's going to be a lot of thunder and lightning. It's the biggest hurricane I ever saw."

Between these urgent warnings, Steven, with the help of Todd, began to negotiate with the teacher the making of a hurricane. They decided that they wanted the lights in the room to be flicked on and off to simulate lightning, and "something very loud" for thunder. They settled on a metal pot cover and metal spoon from the kitchen. When all was ready, catastrophic warnings by Steven began: "This is the worse hurricane on earth. The wind is shaking the Empire State building. The fish are drowning in the rain. Some people, too." Steven stood on a chair orchestrating the entire event. At his direction the teacher flicked the lights, Todd resoundingly banged the pot cover. The area vibrated with activity. All children were quickly taken indoors. "Champion swimmer doctors" from the hospital saved those who fell into the water. Small sailboats zigzagged in the ocean and crashed into islands. In the midst of all this, Amy said, "Could we turn the lights on? I think it's going to rain."

The storm ended. Seaweed was to be found everywhere. Fish were in the hospital and at the airport. The ferry was overturned and the schedule floated in the ocean. There were reunions and the telling of stories of heroism. Yvonne looked around the area. Rolling her eyes, she exclaimed, "BOY, we *really* have to clean up today!!" Steven beamed.

REFLECTING ON THE EXPERIENCE

Beginning the discussion on Monday of the following week, Bill said, "Well. I don't think we should have islands again because it's too hard to get around. You're not so free." Several children nodded.

There is no question that the island block scheme was a compelling experience for the group and that the hurricane of the last day was *an* experience for each person involved, children and teacher. The potency and vividness of the experiences of that week were evident in remarks made by children at various times during the weeks and months that followed. Like survivors who had experienced a natural catastrophe, they talked of "the storm": "Remember when the wind turned the ferry over?" or used it as common knowledge, as in the remark, "You have to have a bridge here.

People can't swim a very big river. They can't swim from an island to an island. Same thing." The events of the week were a shared common experience and a point of reference for individuals and the group to such a degree that sometimes it seemed that what was being remembered was an actual natural event rather than a drama they had created. The emerging and pervading qualities of the situations of that week were grasped by and responded to by each child. There were truly few "seams" and "unfilled blanks." The events brought Dewey's description of aesthetic experience to life.

> In an experience, flow is from something to something. As one part leads into another and as one part carries on what went before, each gains distinctness in itself. The enduring whole is diversified by successive phases that are emphases of its varied colors. (AE, 36; LW 10:43)

The wholeness that existed in the dramatic play issued from the total participation of the children. They gave completely of themselves. Their thoughts, feelings, senses, and movement came forth in unity. Particularly in the events of the last day, there was in the children's reactions and activities an "interpenetration of habits," to state it in Deweyan terms, that gave to the event its unity and completeness. Integration prevailed within each person and in the situation. There was wholeness.

Leading to this consummation, there were also many instances of trial and error experimentation, of "starts and stops." At various times, Bill's participation could be characterized in this way. In part, he lacked the experiences that could have informed his functioning. An equally salient factor was that he was consistently open to stimuli, to the distraction of potentially exciting situations with his special friends. Bill's connections to the larger scene often tended to be circumscribed by the immediate pleasures of the moment. At the same time, it was Bill who made the remark the following week that in island life "you're not so free." The cumulative effect of the experiences of the week, for all of Bill's disconnected moments, had led him to a fundamental understanding. In his own way and time, he had meaningfully pieced together his experiencing.

Yvonne's functioning within the block play was narrowed by her falling back on habituated responses. She did not stretch herself. Yvonne's frequently built school was an ongoing theme with few variations in that changing contexts minimally influenced the content of her play. Another significant influence for this child was time, the time she needed to allow herself fuller interaction with the larger social context. Yvonne tended to limit her interactions to the immediate environment she created, leaving the larger social setting as a taken-for-granted, undifferentiated background. Her irritation and impatience, which tended to surface so quickly, and her unwillingness to discomfort herself for any length of time, brought closure to situations too soon. In *Art as Experience,* Dewey speaks of the linkage of past and present in the experiential continuum and of the "gaps" that may occur. The observations seem particularly fitting to Yvonne's attitude and activity and offer a way of perceiving and understanding her participation.

> There is always a gap between the here and now of direct interaction and the past interactions whose funded result constitutes the meanings with which we grasp and understand what is now occurring. Because of this gap, all conscious perception involves a risk; it is a venture into the unknown, for as it assimilates the present to the past it also brings about some reconstruction of that past. When past and present fit exactly into one another, when there is only recurrence, complete uniformity, the resulting experience is routine and mechanical; it does not come to consciousness in perception. The inertia of habit overrides adaptation of the meaning of the here and now with that of experiences, without which there is no consciousness, the imaginative phase of experience. (AE, 272; LW 10:276–277)

For many of the children the idea of the entire floor being an ocean with islands was a rather exotic and quite abstract context in which to work. (Actually, all the children lived on an island–the island of Manhattan in New York City–but their understanding of this fact was primarily on a verbal level.) For some of the children, their functioning in the first few days was a constant encountering of unexpected obstacles and surprises. They had to contend with the fact that they could not walk on water, and if they wanted to go from place to place they had to arrange to do so. They were literally surrounded by an ocean of problems, which many initially avoided or denied. By observing the functioning of some of their peers who could deal with this novel context, such as Todd, and with the support of the teacher, who added structure and information when needed, what had started as a confusing, somewhat disorienting context gradually began to take form. The encounter with the conditions of island life through their dramatic play, even with its existing limitations and artificiality, was an experiencing of what life on an island would be like for the children because they responded to the detail of that reality. Through interaction with the created conditions, they experienced *islandness* and came to understand, in varying degrees, its meaning and implications. To concretize some of their questions and ideas, stories were read and research initiated that led to some children making models of islands–plasticene forms in aluminum trays that were then filled with water. As Amy worked on her model, she noted, "See, you can't swim under an island. Not even fish; they have to go around too. (pause) Do fish know about islands?" New questions and ideas literally surfaced.

In their interactions with each other and with the settings they had created, the children engaged in the social construction of knowledge. In their discussions and activities they had the opportunity to participate in the construction of common, shared knowns, to perceive themselves as knowing and capable of directing and contributing to their search for understanding. The experiences of the week generated considerable interest in transportation, which then led to trips, research, discussions, and the working out of ideas in the block area. Possibly, the interest in transportation dovetailed with the children's increasing desire for independence and figuring out how one makes one's way in the world. Jeff, who had contributed little to discussions during the week of islands, explained the topic of transportation to another child with, "O.K., so, if it's too far to walk, how do you get there? I mean anywhere—your grandma or even into space. *That's* what we're trying to find out."

Over the course of a week, the activities in the block area offered children multiple opportunities for reflection. In the problems that emerged daily, children encountered unsettlement in the form of doubt, confusion, conflict as they tried to deal with the ocean/island environment and each other. Observing their interrelated activities, one is reminded of Dewey's active and passive phases of experiencing.

> To "learn from experience" is to make a backward and forward connection between what we do to things and what we enjoy and suffer from things in consequence. Under such conditions, doing becomes a trying; an experiment with the world to find out what it is like; the undergoing becomes an instruction—the discovery of the connection of things. (DE, 140; MW 9:147)

The shuttling between experimentation and discovery was evident from the first day beginning with the children's attempt to locate themselves within a context and in building a structure. To the usual problems found in construction—contending with the physical properties of wooden blocks while also attempting to give form to an idea through the medium— an additional element was introduced. The children had to deal with the fact that their respective structures existed in a novel and problem-producing environment. While building, they had to think about whether the particular context would affect construction and content. While Amy was building her hospital, she wondered aloud, "How do you use an ambulance in the ocean?" In other hospitals she had built, ambulance service was a taken-for-granted feature. In the absence of familiar roads, the taken-for-granted became a question.

It is in the dramatic play complementing block building that the opportunities for reflection multiply further. To use Dewey's formulation, dramatic play may be seen as that shuttling "backward and forward" to make connections. The resulting chain effect of action-change spreads into an ever-widening network in a group setting as children interact and create cause-effect situations for each other. Dramatic play becomes an arena in which each child brings his or her own world of personal meaning and, in encounter with others, has an opportunity to examine, amend, and order that world. Knowns and information are tried and tested, and so are feelings.

In operating the weather station, Steven had found a fresh opening for his interest in power as he controlled the movements and actions of the group through his hurricane. His experiment with power occurred within the self-created boundaries of play, which have a beginning and end and in which participation is self-regulated. In externalizing feelings in a situation created by oneself, and that contains selected elements of one's experience, the child has an opportunity to distance feelings and in the doing make them more accessible to examination and understanding. Dramatic play offers a vehicle for the interplay of reality and phantasy, the objective and subjective. As doing and reflecting reciprocally inform each other, the child is also shuttling between self and world, and within self. As children "experiment with the world to find out what it is like," they make selections and connections and construct meaning.

Confronting the problematic in a reasoned, ordered manner comes within the realm of possibilities for children when the situation is grounded within and connected to their experience. In such instances they are able to participate in a rudimentary form of the process of inquiry—a possibility often denied them in theory. Acting within the situations that evolve it is necessary for the child to observe, analyze, hypothesize, and make connections because the world has widened beyond personal boundaries in a group setting. As boundaries stretch, they help to reveal gaps in understanding and information. As children attempt resolution of the problematic, their structures are there to refer to as grounding points of reflection. A tangible reference point exists to which one may return for review and reconstruction. Steven could see why his fish store was going out of business.

Time as measure is not a typical concern of young children except in interaction with adults. Yet it became a real and significant factor with the appearance of the ferry in the ocean community. In their brief encounter with schedules came the dawning realization that clocks, numbers, time are means for ordering. In discussion and in their interrelated activities the social nature of time entered their thinking. Children are capable of dealing with complexity when it appears in a form relevant to their experiencing and in situations where they are active participants and contributors. The concept of time was made a bit less mysterious and remote when the children had to deal with it concretely in relation to their activities. These encounters are initiations into the ordered world of knowledge. They are the times of "getting the feel of it," qualitative openings into the larger world the child is trying to understand.

In the anecdotal material presented in this chapter, blocks and dramatic play offered the children a unique opportunity to view situations from a panoramic vantage point. They could stand at any point and view the entire undertaking, observing its detail, the relationship of parts to the whole, and the interactions that evolved. In encountering dilemmas they could reflect, review, hypothesize, imagine, and not get lost because the issue at hand, the topic for thought, was tangibly present. As Susan Isaacs (1966) observed, "Verbal thinking can hardly yet be *sustained* in its own right, in the earlier years. It draws its vitality from the actual problems of concrete understanding and of manipulation in which it takes its rise, and the solution of which it furthers" (pp. 84–85).

IMAGINATION

Permeating the material discussed in this chapter, both Dewey's philosophical examination of experience and the implications for education, is the presence of imagination. Although not discussed explicitly, imagination is a qualitative force that moves experience and keeps habit vitally plastic. Imagination is the means by which past and present become meaningfully connected and the unknown future becomes related to the here and now. It is the qualitative element that makes possible the transformation and reconstruction of experience.

> [Imagination] designates a quality that animates and pervades all processes of making and observation. It is a *way* of seeing and feeling things as they compose an integral whole. It is the large and generous blending of interests at the point where the mind comes in contact with the world. When the old and familiar things are made new in experience, there is imagination. When the new is created, the far and strange become the most natural inevitable things in the world. There is always some measure of adventure in the meeting of mind and universe, and this adventure is, in its measure, imagination. (AE, 267; LW 10:271–272)

Teachers are repeatedly exhorted to support, nourish, and encourage imagination. Teachers' guides frequently contain activities (usually supplementary to the main purpose) designed to "encourage imagination and creativity." More often than not, such supplementary activities suggest the use of some art material and, all too frequently, also direct the content. Such standardized, contrived responses are not using imagination as Dewey intends. To encourage and nourish imagination is a difficult task. Part of the difficulty lies in the intangibility of that which is to be nourished. It is not like concrete facts or content that can be held on to, offered, or presented. That which is to be nourished is a possession of the other. What we may offer are the conditions inviting its use, opportunities wherein the child may suspend the old and familiar for what has never been before. It is an invitation to a world of "suppose," "if," and "maybe." It is a personal place of insights, humor, and fresh connections. In play, children unselfconsciously use it, and stretch beyond the here and now in contact with the world. To imagine is to possess power—to transform, to change the given.

The use of blocks in a group setting where children are free to bring their own interests and questions into play is one such opportunity. Blocks have been used illustratively because they offer so many varied, open-ended possibilities for imagination for individuals and the group. The dramatic play that evolves in these situations invites children into the fullness of experiencing indicated by Dewey. In a group setting, blocks and dramatic play make significant communication possible and give rise to a sense of community. With time—the time to experiment, pause, try again, and discover with the various materials they have used to construct and communicate—children move gradually from their world of personal symbols to use symbols shared with and understood by others and to write their stories.

Unstructured materials and activities that encourage children to freely give of themselves invite expression, communication, and the imaginative reconstruction of experience. The labeling of materials and activities for the purpose of description and analysis, may be undermining to the sense of wholeness being sought in the curriculum. An unwanted, subtle dichotomizing may be engendered reminiscent of traditional polarizations of affect and intellect, play and work, art and science. The point to be made is that imagination, a qualitative "way of seeing and feeling," should be kept alive in all the activities taking place in a classroom, whether they are structured or unstructured, teacher- or child-directed. The affective and the intellectual, the aesthetic and the scientific inform and lead into each other. The either/or perspective is of our making, an adult enterprise imposed on the spirit and imagination of children's activities and vision.

To create and maintain the conditions that will promote children's imaginative adventuring into the world, asks that we be willing to chance this adventure through our own risk-taking and venturing into the unknown. The task may be harder for us because we have had the time to taste the comfort and security seemingly available in "certainties and guarantees" in a changing world. We are also aware that our world is of our making in larger measure than we may admit, and one may wish, even for a brief time, to deny the possibility of choice. Yet, when we do choose, if our choices tend toward qualitative venturing into a world that does not hold the guarantee of predetermined guidelines written for faceless teachers and standardized children, we need sustenance for the journey, for it is difficult and often lonely – a paradox because in teaching one is always with others. It is in the community of storytellers – in our teacher talk – as we listen to each other's dilemmas, pose questions to think about, laugh, imagine, and reflect together, through the sharing of our teaching self, that we revitalize ourselves. Teaching is too hard to do alone. Teacher talk moves soliloquy into dialogue, and in anticipating together we deepen understanding and find new possibilities in self and in our doing.

RELATED READINGS

Griffiths, R. (1935). *Imagination in early childhood*. London: Routledge & Kegan Paul.

Lowenfeld, M. (1967). *Play in childhood*. New York: Wiley Science Editions.

Monighan-Nourot, P., Scales, B., Van Hoorn, J. L., & Almy, M. (1987). *Looking at children's play: The bridge from theory to practice*. New York: Teachers College Press.

8

Challenge and Commitment

I admit gladly that the new education is *simpler* than the old. . . . But the easy and the simple are not identical. To discover what is really simple and to act upon the discovery is an exceedingly difficult task. The process is a slow and arduous one. It is a matter of growth, and there are many obstacles which tend to obstruct growth and to deflect it into wrong lines.

(EE, 30; LW 13:14–15)

The preceding chapters have presented a view of the person – the social individual – and an examination of the concept of experience from a Deweyan perspective. Ideas about the nature of the person and the variety in experience were connected to daily classroom life. In shuttling back and forth between theory and practice, between ideas and their meaning, some guiding principles were presented, with the understanding that principles are neither rules nor prescriptions but "tools for dealing with new situations, methods for solving problems" (Rucker, 1972, p. 115).

With Dewey as guide, rather than embarking on a set itinerary or possessing a map to a promised land, we are offered an invitation to journey. We are told that the terrain is changing, precarious, and unstable. Rather than impediment, these conditions are to serve as catalysts, challenging opportunities to use our potential and capacity to grow, to expand our perspective and enrich experience, and in the process to create and shape the place where we would like to be. Also present to guide the journey is Dewey's vision of a democratic society, a place where diverse voices find commonality and expression through communication and shared purpose. How much sustenance can be derived from Dewey's ideas and vision for the journey that is teaching? What are the difficulties?

There can be no general answer to these questions for each response reflects a history of experiences – of individual starting points, of moments of connecting and meaning making, times of ownership of ideas. For myself, making sense of Dewey was a way of making sense of teaching, a way to question practice in the search for coherence and integrity in my work. The habits of mind and heart with which I came to teaching, attitudes rooted in my life, family, and culture, predisposed me to wanting to know *why* I did *what* I did. As a child, acting and being in the world was a search to find out how things worked and also why they worked that way. Being bilingual made these forays into experiencing more complex and interesting because I had two scripts from which to speak and act. From this dual perspective I intuited that there were different ways of making sense of the world, different *whys* for the same situation. With my child's view of the world I reduced understanding to a simple explanation: Reasons depended on the storyteller—the reason-maker—and reasons depended on what each person believed to be "good" or "bad." With time, the narrow mind-set of good and bad was expanded and new words were introduced: *right, wrong, truth, opinion, theory, ideology*. What lingered in this process of change was the earlier intuition—the presence of a reason-maker and the existence of choice. In contrast to childhood, where choice is often a theoretical matter, adulthood consistently presents situations where choice is required. And, in choosing, self is declared, given form, and transformed.

Teaching is a way of being who we are and a place where in our actions we make manifest what we believe and value. Teaching is a way of rehearsing and trying identity, of creating and discovering self. In teaching, self is constantly elicited, always on call, responding. There is an alertness required, an alertness to understand each situation, the meaning and possibilities of the present moment, an alertness that throws us back to self, to our reason-making. Having Dewey enter my teaching was similar to listening to and trying to have a conversation with a reason-maker of teaching, to hear another story about teaching, and while listening, to compare, contrast, question, and try out reasons for my teaching. The conversation between us—my thoughts and questions posed to Dewey's printed words—did not always flow easily. While I grasped that the philosophy he offered made the giving of rules and prescriptions impossible, I sometimes wanted answers, especially when the concrete situations of the classroom seemed overwhelming.

My frustration in such moments was not unique. I encounter the same dilemmas in the classrooms of the teachers with whom I work and in the courses I teach. We all struggle to make sense of our actions and to find the *whys* that go deeper than what works for the moment. It is a struggle because what Dewey asks is our continued growth, reflection, intelligence, imagination, and the risk-taking and responsibility involved in creating both curriculum and our teaching self. In the absence of absolutes and directives, Dewey asks the teacher to suspend the need for certainty, to accept the responsibility of freedom and choice, and to view self as capable of creating. This requires courage, initiative, a defined sense of purpose, intelligence, commitment, and perspective, particularly the perspective that is born in hope and laughter.

Some of the difficulties in applying Dewey's thought may be found in the distance each of us may perceive between his view of the teacher and teaching and where we think we are—not unlike the distance we perceive between the real and ideal of democracy. The real of society—the reality of exclusion, inequity, repression, violence, and despair—is far from the ideal. Yet, the ideal is there not as unattainable perfection but to inform the present, to underline what we must attend to, and to help in locating what obstructs the realization of the ideal. An ideal locates the territory of interest and concern, points to desired characteristics and qualities of the landscape, and indicates those features that obstruct the growth of the person and of society. The informing of the real by the ideal focuses the work to be done to lessen the distance between the two. Dewey's portrait of the teacher outlines the attitudes, intelligence, and commitment required for teaching-learning and it is not surprising that these qualities are essential to sustaining a democratic society.

THE PROBLEMATIC

With such a prolific writer, how does one create a whole from the varied parts? How does one follow Dewey as he expands ideas, adds further detail, and chooses yet another vantage point from which to view experience, the social individual, education, and society? There is no set itinerary. Each is a personal story of discoveries, connections, and experiencing. My own journey had many starts and stops, detours, and lengthy pauses. What I sought were responses to my questions, dilemmas born in my experience. The journey became an adventure as I moved beyond *Experience and Education* and other educational writings to broader philosophical works such as *Art as Experience, Experience and Nature,* and to *Human Nature and Conduct, The Public and Its Problems,* and Dewey's essays on varied topics, and as I worked to give form to and apply what I had synthesized. With time I came to see and think of Dewey's philosophy as a whole made up of parts that were never truly separate from the whole. Parts were interconnected by an elastic thread. Pulling out a part of the whole to view it more closely, attracted and brought other parts closer.

Any movement caused tension, expansions and contractions, within the whole. Pulling out "experience," a rather large part, automatically drew other parts—habit, quality, interaction, growth. Each in turn then provoked movement in other parts, seemingly far afield, such as intelligence, ends-in-view, valuation. It was when I was able to hold one part for closer examination while consciously aware of the elastic thread that held it to the whole and when I acknowledged the resultant tensions, that I found firmer ground and could translate Dewey's ideas into practice in a variety of circumstances. If that thread is to be named, for me it is the *social individual.* The thread must be elastic because Dewey's philosophy rejects absolutes and boundaries, and elasticity allows for the uniqueness of individual styles of searching. And in all the reflecting, synthesizing, acting, and trying that results from reading, discussing, and thinking about Dewey's ideas, it is important to remember that the whole one creates from Dewey's philosophy is a *part* of the whole that is self.

While Dewey cautions that "the process is a long and arduous one," I believe that I read those words lightly, on the surface. In Dewey I found principles, guidance, a view of human nature, of learning and growth, and a broad vision of a democratic society that connected with my preferred possibilities. But there were also times when I felt overwhelmed with all that I had to consider. Actually, it was not the *all* that created pressure, it was the moral tone, the whispered *should,* that I heard in his words that caused tension. I sense the same tension in the faces and questions of students in courses when we talk of issues of equity, when questions are raised that connect individual classrooms to society, or when the values of society are questioned. What makes the process long and arduous is not Dewey's what—his view of growth and learning. It is his *what for,* the sense of purpose, the moral sense that permeates the whole, that is difficult. Everything one does, each choice, connects with and is part of a larger vision and purpose.

With his unfailing purposefulness, Dewey begins with a taken-for-granted headstart while many of us are still at the qualitative stage of sensing, of feeling purpose. Purpose requires personal time to grow. Like mind, purpose emerges; it is not ready made. A sense of purpose, if it is to be meaningful and unified rather than a collection of givens delivered by others, is a personal achievement. It is not Dewey's sense of purpose that is questioned but the tempo of his purposefulness. Working within the framework he offers, as one searches for meaning, meaning that informs and fuels purpose, it is important to acknowledge and be aware of one's own inner rhythm and the need for revitalizing pauses. Time is needed to select, to transform words into action, to experience ideas, to make philosophy one's own, and to choose the responsibility and commitment that come with the larger purpose and vision implicit in Dewey's philosophy.

To further ease the tempo of the energetic Dewey, to personalize it, it is helpful when thinking of Dewey's omnipresent connections and continuities, to understand (and accept) that it is simply not possible that every connection will be made, or that continuity will occur with each opportunity offered. Again, time is needed for connections to be made, children's personal time of playing, feeling, thinking, and imagining, and teachers' personal time of observing, reflecting, imagining, and questioning. Connections and continuity, like interaction, are principles to be remembered, not directives to be enforced. Nor are these concepts to be diminished by surface connections, the appearance of integration.

EXPERIENCING THE CHALLENGE OF DEMOCRACY

Several questions have been raised. Among them: Does the social atmosphere of the classroom invite all stories to be told? And, in learning about the world, which complexities, which issues, do *we* bring into the classroom? Taken together, the two questions speak to the partnership between children and teachers in the development of curriculum. Looking at the history of early education there have been diverse answers to these same questions. For example, reviewing the curriculum for young children at Dewey's Laboratory School in Chicago at the turn of the century, the early progressives turned their attention away from the universal truths and spirituality of the Froebelian kindergartens to the real world of people's jobs – the occupations – and toward finding the connections and interdependencies among people and the world in which they lived. Children learned about the world of the carpenter through trips, discussions, and their own carpentry. Food was talked about, planted, cooked, and shared. The worlds of home and work were brought into the classroom to be examined, connected, played, and constructed. Through their active participation children made sense of the world, that part of the world that teachers invited into the classroom.

Parts of that legacy remain in the curriculum of early education in the studies of home, family, community workers and services, food, and transportation. We still take trips to the post office and the police and fire stations, to which we have added trips to recycling centers. We continue to plant and cook and we have diversified the foods we eat to include more tastes and cultures. In the "experiment with the world to find out what it is like" we take children out into the world to see, to touch, to smell, to hear, to taste its multiple textures and colors. Asking how much of the world we invite *into* our classrooms does not mean do police officers, postal carriers, construction workers, or parents come into the classroom to share their skills and craft. What is asked is whether homelessness, poverty, AIDS, drugs, and the "isms" of our society—as real as trips to the post office—are welcome in our classrooms. Does Dewey offer guidance for these questions?

Dewey's concept of a democratic society, both the community of the classroom and the Great Community that is to be society, is built on communication, participation, and association. His vision of democracy welcomes plurality and diversity and rejects barriers that divide and exclude. Accepting the spirit of Dewey's vision, we are challenged to attend to whatever diminishes the growth of a democratic society and to whatever silences voices, voices needed for participation and communication and vital to a growing community. In essays written in the 1920s and during the Depression, Dewey spoke of the failings and shortcomings of education when schools presented idealized images of society to students, images that neglected understanding of political power and of the social and economic forces working beneath the surface of society. In some of these essays he spoke of the "innocence" with which students leave school only to be surprised abruptly by the realities of society. In Dewey's words about innocence written many decades ago I find similarity to attitudes prevalent today when social issues are raised in relation to early childhood curriculum. I see a connection between a concern with innocence in the past and the priority and attention given frequently to development today.

The reliance on developmental theory in determining and shaping curriculum has a long history in early education. In a variety of ways development often has become a philosophy of education, serving as the *what for* of curriculum for young children. Where once we may have spoken of preserving the innocence of childhood when selecting what parts of the world to bring into the classroom, today we speak of what is developmentally appropriate. It is a phrase that evokes mixed feelings: my willingness to give attention to development and my resistance to the judgment implicit in the word *appropriate*. Whose view of development? Who decides? Is it not clearer, more accurate, to speak of having a developmental perspective or orientation, or being "mindful" of development?

In the desire to protect childhood innocence, not wishing to burden the young, we shape children's vision and their view of the world. In our protective caring, we tend to underestimate children's capacities and abilities and to overlook their wish to understand and to make sense of the world in which they live. Directly and indirectly, children encounter and are shaped by the "isms" of society because they live in the society, not apart from it. Their encounters raise many questions, evoke thoughts and feelings, and children are expert in sensing when and whether adults want to hear their questions and concerns. Regardless of adult hesitancy, there are times when social issues arrive unexpectedly, as occurred one morning in Lee's kindergarten classroom as children were discussing birthdays. At one point, with a touch of humor, Lee asked the children, "Is there anyone who doesn't have a birthday?" The response was surprising and poignant and an example of children's thinking about their encounters in the world. A child answered, "Homeless people don't have birthdays. They have no place to have the cake."

Lee could have dropped this topic with some surface response or decided that it was too complicated for the children to understand. Or, accepting a rationale often found when considering social issues in relation to early education, she could have reasoned that since there were no children in the class who were homeless the topic was not relevant. Lee chose to explore the children's understanding of the world and asked them to talk about what they knew of homelessness. They knew a great deal and there was diversity in the information they possessed. At one point in the discussion, one child lay on the floor and said, "I'm homeless." Words were insufficient to explain his thoughts and feelings. He had to enact the meaning of the word. There was no laughter from the other children, only the nodding of heads in shared recognition. In the weeks that followed, the director of a soup kitchen came to the class to talk about her work and discussions about homelessness continued for many weeks. Lee's willingness to step into unchartered territory not included in her curriculum guide honored the children's thinking and their desire to understand. What happened is also an example of the partnership that can exist between children and teachers in the development of curriculum when the social atmosphere of the classroom welcomes questioning and the telling of personal stories. But the question that has been raised goes beyond the unexpected.

In a 1936 address at a regional conference of the Progressive Education Association Dewey spoke of the relationship between schools and democracy, and of the challenge democracy poses for education. In his talk he made certain distinctions among the words *knowledge, understanding,* and *information.* He noted that "knowledge to so many people means 'information.'" For Dewey such knowledge, "information about things," is static. "There is no guarantee in any amount of information, even if skillfully conveyed, that an intelligent attitude of mind will be formed" or that it will lead to understanding and intelligent action (CDE, LW:11). For Dewey, understanding and action are connected. To understand something is to know how it works and to be able to *make* it work (p.

184). The distinctions noted in relation to knowledge, information, and understanding are reminiscent of the differences found between recognition and perception.

All these distinctions are pertinent to the question of what parts of the world we bring into the classroom. Too often we deny through silence, or settle for information and "knowns" about democracy and struggle, instead of seeking understanding that requires the examination of attitudes and the transformation and change of habits. An example of these distinctions is my experience in the past few years as I visit classrooms of young children in January and hear the story of Rosa Parks. Too often it sounds like a fairy tale about a tired woman who sat down in a bus, because missing are both the context of the story and the detail of Rosa Parks's life of activism. In such oversimplification the power and the lesson of human struggle are diminished as well as the possibility of discovering connections to self. In fairy tales change occurs magically. In life it is not magic that creates change but the commitment and struggles of people–individuals acting alone and collectively over time to change the given. How we present the world to children shapes their vision of the world and their place in it. Dewey offers a succinct statement of our task. "The crucial question is the extent to which the material of the social studies . . . is taught simply as information about present society or is taught in connection with things that are done, that need to be done, and how to do them" (CDE, LW:11).

"Things that are done" points to learning about power and powerlessness, about exclusion and privilege, and the "isms" of society. "That need to be done" points to the conscious and principled examination of the social atmosphere in which children work, of the materials used and the knowledge offered, of the images and ideas presented daily, of the nature of the invitation we extend to children when they enter our classrooms. "How to do them" brings us to action.

Anti-Bias Curriculum: Tools for Empowering Young Children (1989) by Louise Derman-Sparks and the A.B.C. Task Force is an example of an approach to curriculum that accepts the challenge that democracy presents to education. The balancing of the social and psychological is accomplished with exceptional skill and power. The world of young children is dynamically present as is the aim of the curriculum: "at heart anti-bias curriculum is about social change" (p. x). Anti-bias is defined as

> An active/activist approach to challenging prejudice, stereotyping, bias, and the "isms." In a society in which institutional structures create and maintain sexism, racism, and handicappism, it is not sufficient to be non-biased (and also highly unlikely), nor is it sufficient to be an observer. It is necessary for

each individual to actively intervene, to challenge and counter the personal and institutional behaviors that perpetuate oppression. (p. 3)

In the authors' definition of anti-bias we are reminded of Dewey's "philosophy is thinking what the known demands of us."

The strength of the *Anti-Bias Curriculum* lies in its organic approach. What is offered permeates the whole of curriculum. It is a perspective, a way of seeing and teaching that becomes a part of each day, of each activity, a constant companion in our inner conversations as we make choices throughout the day. And in its genuine understanding of classroom life and teaching, it invites teacher talk as a way of learning, of assessing mistakes and experimental trying, of sharing doubts and accomplishments. A further strength (and support) of this approach to curriculum is that the authors confront directly and honestly the difficulties to be encountered, the "long and arduous process" the approach entails: the tensions and disagreements that may surface; the necessary and often painful self-examination; the continuing dialogue with parents; and the ongoing hard work, the time and commitment required. What is clearly evident in this curriculum is a deep understanding of children, of family and community life, and of the meaning of communication, participation, and association in supporting and maintaining a democratic classroom and society.

The Public and the Personal

There is a need to pause and respond qualitatively in this discussion about confronting racism, sexism, disability, heterosexism, and classism and the place of homelessness, AIDS, drugs, and poverty in the curriculum. Issues, "isms," curriculum can be distancing words unless we also remember that we are talking about people, of the actual lives of many children who experience the "topics" of discussion. Are these stories, painful stories, welcome in the classroom? How may a public setting such as the classroom welcome personal concerns? Openness in classroom time and space — the way we arrange and furnish the environment, how we offer and extend time — is one part of the invitation. The other is the social atmosphere where children may experience trust: trust in adults who act fairly and empathically; who listen with care; who are consistent in their support and do not turn away; who understand how to surface and support personal interests that lead to mastery and learning and a sense of worth. The invitation also exists in the time and space we create for children's play, for discussions about how they perceive the world, for the telling and writing of stories, and the opportunities we create for both private times and group times, and times of shared work that can lead to a sense of community. Public places can be distant and overwhelming. They can also feel personal and safe. What they become depends very much on what we, the adults, make them through our humanity, the caring and understanding we express, and the responsibility we choose to assume.

Trust, acceptance, support, and invitations are not only for children. Adults also need the time and space to talk about what they do, to give voice to their concerns, to raise their questions, to wonder about possibilities. The time for talk, for sharing, cannot be left to chance or be incidental. We need it as an ongoing part of our professional lives. And that includes time for parents to talk about their children, about their aspirations and values, and about the struggles and joys of parenting for they are an essential part of the partnership involved in teaching.

Surfacing and making explicit the challenges that democracy poses for the educator increase the complexities of teaching. When we consider each "*what* shall I do," we are challenged to connect to the *what for* of our work, to the reason-making of our teaching. In recent years many educators in early education have situated the work of democracy in the concept of multiculturalism. In the various approaches to and interpretations of the meaning of multiculturalism (Sleeter & Grant, 1987) there is a tendency to focus on recognizing and accepting our pluralism and diversity, but these approaches do not always go on to make further connections, connections that address directly the political and moral nature of the work needed to achieve a democratic society. Respecting and celebrating the surface richness and texture of society are necessary and important, but at the same time we cannot neglect attending to what binds us together. What do we choose and declare as our common purpose and shared work? Where do we create the openings for the communication, the participation and associated living that democracy requires? A vision is not a blueprint. It does not contain all the details necessary to build a structure. But neither is it merely a dream. A vision is realized through our active participation in the reality of the present moment, in the conditions that exist now and must be confronted now—and *now* is present in each new day. What gives strength and reality to a vision is built on the detail of what we choose to confront, to question, and to act to change in *and* out of the classroom.

WRITING THIS BOOK has been a process of remembering and of re-experiencing classroom teaching, of reliving that world while also standing outside of it in the act of writing. What has helped to sustain the effort have been the teachers with whom I work, the children in the classrooms I visit, the genuine searching and questioning of students in the courses I teach, and the conversations with colleagues who share the work of being teachers of teachers.

Unfolding and connecting Dewey's thought, sharing the whole I created from his philosophy of education, reaffirms my belief in the importance to teaching of a consciously held and examined philosophical framework. For me John Dewey has been a teacher who has guided, who has offered principles, who has inspired through his broad vision of a democratic society and his understanding of experience in all its nuance, and who also did not have answers to many of my questions. His philosophy is about possibilities rather than certainties. What would or could be realized depended on my reflection, my actions, my choices, my commitment. That placed me in the position of initiator rather than follower. It asked me to imagine what I could be.

> Choice sustains a double relation to the self. It reveals the existing self and it forms the future self. That which is chosen is that which is found congenial to the desires and habits of the self as it already exists . . . every choice is at the forking of the roads, and the path chosen shuts off certain opportunities and opens others. . . . Superficially, the deliberation which terminates in choice is concerned with weighing the values of particular ends. Below the surface, it is a process of discovering what sort of being a person most wants to be. (TML, 149; LW 7:286–287)

The social individual with whom this book began is an open-ended possibility. What we do in our classrooms, the view we offer of the world, the choices we make, add detail and direction to possibility–for the children, ourselves, and society. And in our choosing, in that "process of discovering," we find that in teaching, the personal, the political, the moral, and the aesthetic are interwoven–an understanding that makes it both harder and easier to teach.

RELATED READINGS

Casper, V., Schultz, S., & Wickens, E. (1992, Fall). Breaking the silences: Lesbian and gay parents and the schools. *Teachers College Record, 94*(1), 108–137.

Cheng, C. W., Brizendine, E., & Oakes, J. (1981). What is an "equal chance" for minority children? In J. A. Banks (Ed.), *Education in the 80's: Multiethnic education* (pp. 140–161). Washington, DC: National Education Associates.

Counts, G. S. (1982). Dare the school build a new social order? Carbondale: Southern Illinois University Press, Arcturas Books. (Originally published 1932).

Cuffaro, H. K. (1975, September). Reevaluating basic premises: Curricula free of sexism. *Young Children, 30*(6), 469–478.

Klein, T., Bittel, C., & Molnar, J. (1993, September). No place to call home: Supporting the needs of homeless children in the early childhood classroom. *Young Children, 48*(6), 22–39.

Shapiro, J., Kramer, S., & Hunerberg, C. (1981). *Equal their chances: Children's activities for non-sexist learning.* Englewood Cliffs, NJ: Prentice-Hall.

Williams, L. R., & De Gaetano, Y. (1985). *ALERTA: A multicultural, bilingual approach to teaching young children.* Menlo Park, CA: Addison-Wesley.

Bibliography
Index
About the Author

Bibliography

WRITINGS BY DEWEY

In the listing below of Dewey's writings, the letter codes used in this text to identify the sources of the quotations from Dewey are followed by the title of the appropriate work and full bibliographic information. At the end of each entry, using letter codes in brackets, I have identified the corresponding volume from *The Collected Works of John Dewey*, all edited by Jo Ann Boydston and published by Southern Illinois University Press. The copyright date of the volume used in this text is included within the brackets. It should be noted that some volumes of *The Collected Works* have been issued in both hard cover and paperback editions. As the two editions were published at different times, the copyright dates for the same volume will differ. The 34 volumes are divided as follows:

EW *The Early Works, 1882–1898*
MW *The Middle Works, 1899–1924*
LW *The Later Works, 1925–1953*

AE *Art as experience*. New York: G. P. Putnam's Sons, Capricorn Books, 1958. (Originally published, Minton Balch, 1934.) [LW:10, 1989]
CDE The challenge of democracy to education. *The Later Works, 1925–1953*. Vol.14: 1935–1937. Edited by Jo Ann Boydston. Carbondale: Southern Illinois University Press, 1991.
CC *The child and the curriculum*. In M. S. Dworkin (Ed.), *Dewey on education*. New York: Teachers College Press, 1959. (Originally published, University of Chicago Press, 1902.) [MW:2, 1976]
CE "Consciousness" and experience. In J. J. McDermott (Ed.), *The philosophy of John Dewey: Vol. 1. The structure of experience*. New York: G. P. Putnam's Sons, Capricorn Books, 1973. (Originally published 1899.) [MW:1, 1983]
CD Creative democracy–The task before us. *The Later Works, 1925–1953*. Vol. 14: 1935–1937. Edited by Jo Ann Boydston. Carbondale: Southern Illinois University Press, 1991.
DE *Democracy and education*. New York: Free Press, 1966. (Originally published 1916.) [MW:9, 1985]
EE *Experience and education*. New York: Collier Books, 1963. (Originally published 1938.) [LW:13, 1991]

EN   *Experience and nature*. New York: La Salle, IL: Open Court, 1929. (Originally published 1925.) [LW:1, 1988]

HWT   *How we think: A restatement of the relation of reflective thinking to the educative process*. Lexington, MA: D. C. Heath, 1933. [LW:8, 1989]

HNC   *Human nature and conduct*. New York: Random House, 1930. (Originally published, Henry Holt, 1922.) [MW:14, 1988]

IE   *Interest and effort in education*. Carbondale: Southern Illinois University Press, Arcturus Books, 1975. (Originally published, Houghton Mifflin, 1913.) [MW:7]

LTI   *Logic: The theory of inquiry*. New York: Henry Holt, 1938. [LW:12, 1991]

MPE   *Moral Principles in Education*. Carbondale: Southern Illinois University Press, Arcturus Books, 1975. (Originally published, Houghton Mifflin, 1909.) [MW:4, 1977]

PC   My pedagogic creed. In M. S. Dworkin (Ed.), *Dewey on education*. New York: Teachers College Press, 1959. (Originally published, 1897.) [EW:5, 1975]

PIP   *The public and its problems*. Chicago: Swallow Press, 1954. (Originally published, Henry Holt, 1927.) [LW:2, 1984]

QT   Qualitative thought. In R. J. Bernstein (Ed.), *John Dewey on experience, nature, and freedom*. New York: Liberal Arts Press, 1960. (Originally published, 1930.) [LW:5, 1984]

TML   *Theory of the moral life*. New York: Irvington Publishers, 1980. (Originally published, 1908, in *Ethics* by J. Dewey & J. H. Tufts; revised substantially, 1932, Henry Holt.) [LW:7, 1984]

TI   Time and individuality. In R. J. Bernstein (Ed.), *John Dewey on experience, nature, and freedom*. New York: Liberal Arts Press, 1960. (Originally published 1940.) [LW:14, 1991]

EDITED COLLECTIONS OF DEWEY WRITINGS

Bernstein, R. J. (Ed.). (1960). *John Dewey on experience, nature, and freedom*. New York: Liberal Arts Press.

McDermott, J. J. (Ed.). (1973). *The philosophy of John Dewey: Vol. I. The structure of experience*. New York: G. P. Putnam's Sons, Capricorn Books.

McDermott, J. J. (Ed.). (1973). *The philosophy of John Dewey: Vol. II. The lived experience*. New York: G. P. Putnam's Sons, Capricorn Books.

WRITINGS ABOUT DEWEY

Bernstein, R. J. (1966). *John Dewey*. New York: Washington Square Press.

Bernstein, R. J. (1971). *Praxis and action*. Philadelphia: University of Pennsylvania Press.

Boydston, J. (1972). *Guide to the works of John Dewey*. Carbondale: Southern Illinois University Press, Arcturus Books.

Boydston, J., & Poulos, K. (1974). *Checklist of writings about John Dewey 1887–1977* (2nd ed.). Carbondale: Southern Illinois University Press.

Cahn, S. M. (Ed.). (1977). *New studies in the philosophy of John Dewey*. Hanover, NH: University Press of New England.

Coughlan, N. (1975). *Young John Dewey: An essay in American intellectual history*. Chicago: University of Chicago Press.

Dykhuizen, G. (1973). *The life and mind of John Dewey*. Carbondale: Southern Illinois University Press.

Geiger, G. R. (1974). *John Dewey in perspective*. Westport, CT: Greenwood Press.

Gouinlock, J. (Ed.). (1976). *The moral writings of John Dewey: A selection*. New York: Macmillan, Hafner Press.

Hook, S. (1971). *John Dewey: An intellectual portrait*. Westport, CT: Greenwood Press.

Kestenbaum, V. (1977). *The phenomenological sense of John Dewey*. Atlantic Highlands, NJ: Humanities Press.

Morgenbesser, S. (Ed.). (1977). *Dewey and his critics: Essays from the Journal of Philosophy*. New York: The Journal of Philosophy.

Nathanson, J. (1951). *The reconstruction of the democratic life*. New York: Frederick Ungar.

West, C. (1989). *The American evasion of philosophy*. Madison, WI: The University of Wisconsin Press.

Westbrook, R. B. (1991). *John Dewey and American democracy*. Ithaca: Cornell University Press.

Wirth, A. G. (1966). *John Dewey as educator: His design for work in education (1894–1904)*. New York: John Wiley.

REFERENCES AND FURTHER READINGS

Ayers, W. (1989). *The good preschool teacher: Six teachers reflect on their lives*. New York: Teachers College Press.

Berlak, A., & Berlak, H. (1981). *Dilemmas of schooling: Teaching and social change*. London: Methuen.

Biber, B. (1984). *Early education and psychological development*. New Haven, CT: Yale University Press.

Bussis, A. M., Chittenden, E. A., & Amarel, M. (1976). *Beyond surface curriculum*. Boulder, CO: Westview Press.

Carter, K. (1993). The place of story in the study of teaching and teacher education. *Educational Researcher, 22*(1) 5–12.

Clandinin, D. J., & Connelly, F. M. (1992). Teacher as curriculum maker. In P. W. Jackson (Ed.), *Handbook of research on curriculum* (pp. 363–401). New York: Macmillan.

Clark, C. M., & Peterson, P. L. (1986). Teachers' thought processes. In M. Wittrock (Ed.), *Handbook of research on teaching* (3rd ed, pp. 225–296). New York: Macmillan.

Connelly, F. M., & Clandinin, D. J. (1985). Personal practical knowledge and modes of knowing: Relevance for teaching and learning. In E. Eisner (Ed.), *Learning and teaching the ways of knowing* (84th Yearbook, Part 2, NSSE, pp. 174–198). Chicago: University of Chicago Press.

Connelly, F. M., & Clandinin, D. J. (1988). *Teachers as curriculum planners: Narratives of experience*. New York: Teachers College Press.

Connelly, F. M., & Clandinin, D. J. (1990). Studies of experience and narrative inquiry. *Educational Researcher, 19*(4), 2–14.

Cuffaro, H. K. (1982). Unfolding and connecting Dewey's thought from a teacher's perspective. Unpublished dissertation, Teachers College, Columbia University, New York.

Cuffaro, H. K. (1984). Microcomputers in education: Why is earlier better? In D. Sloan (Ed.), *The computer in education: A critical perspective* (pp. 21–30). New York: Teachers College Press.

Derman-Sparks, L., & A. B. C. Task Force. (1989). *Anti-bias curriculum: Tools for empowering young children*. Washington, DC: National Association for the Education of Young Children.

Dewey, J., & Dewey, E. (1962). *Schools of tomorrow*. New York: E. P. Dutton. (Originally published 1915.)

Duckworth, E. (1987). *"The having of wonderful ideas" and other essays on teaching and learning*. New York: Teachers College Press.

Elbaz, F. (1983). *Teacher thinking: A study of practical knowledge*. London: Croom Helm.

Elbaz, F. (1991). Research on teacher's knowledge: The evolution of a discourse. *Journal of Curriculum Studies, 23*(1), 1–20.

Freire, P. (1970). *Pedagogy of the oppressed*. New York: Seabury.

Goodlad, J. I. (1984). *A place called school: Prospects for the future*. New York: McGraw-Hill.

Goodlad, J. I., Klein, M. F., & Associates. (1970). *Behind the classroom door*. Worthington, OH: Charles A. Jones.

Goodlad, J. I., Soder, R., & Sirotnik, K. A. (Eds.). (1990). *The moral dimensions of teaching*. San Francisco: Jossey-Bass.

Hidalgo, N. M., McDowell, C. L., & Siddle, E. V. (1990). *Facing racism in education*. Harvard Educational Review Reprint Series No. 21.

Greene, M. (1973). *Teacher as stranger*. Belmont, CA: Wadsworth.

Greene, M. (1988). *The dialectic of freedom*. New York: Teachers College Press.

Jackson, P. W. (1968). *Life in classrooms*. New York: Holt.

Kozol, J. (1991). *Savage inequalities: Children in America's schools*. New York: Crown.

Lampert, M. (1985). How do teachers manage to teach? Perspectives on problems in practice. *Harvard Educational Review, 55*(2), 178–194.

Lortie, D. (1975). *Schoolteacher*. Chicago: University of Chicago Press.

Paley, V. G. (1979). *White teacher*. Cambridge, MA: Harvard University Press.

Paley, V. G. (1981). *Wally's stories: Conversations in the kindergarten*. Cambridge, MA: Harvard University Press.

Rucker, D. (1972). Dewey's ethics, part two. In J. Boydston (Ed.), *Guide to the works of John Dewey.* Carbondale: Southern Illinois University Press, Arcturus Books.

Schorr, L. B., with Schorr, D. (1989). *Within our reach: Breaking the cycle of disadvantage.* New York: Anchor/Doubleday.

Schubert, W. H. (1991). Teacher lore: A basis for understanding praxis. In C. Witherell & N. Noddings (Eds.), *Stories lives tell: Narrative and dialogue in education* (pp. 207–233). New York: Teachers College Press.

Silin, J. G. (1988). On becoming knowledgeable professionals. In B. Spodek, O. N. Saracho, & D. L. Peters (Eds.), *Professionalism and the early childhood practitioner* (pp. 117–134). New York: Teachers College Press.

Sleeter, C. E., & Grant, C. A. (1987). An analysis of multicultural education in the United States. *Harvard Educational Review, 57*(4), 421–444.

Weiss, L. (Ed.). (1988). *Class, race, and gender in American education.* Albany: State University of New York Press.

Welker, R. (1992). *The teacher as expert: A theoretical and historical perspective.* New York: State University of New York Press.

Witherell, C., & Noddings, N. (Eds.). (1991). *Stories lives tell: Narrative and dialogue in education.* New York: Teachers College Press.

Wood, G. H. (Fall, 1988). Education for democratic empowerment: Educating democratic educators. *Educational Foundations, 2*(3), 37–56.

Yonemura, M. V. (1986). *A teacher at work: Professional development and the early childhood educator.* New York: Teachers College Press.

Index

About the Author

Harriet K. Cuffaro is a member of the graduate faculty at Bank Street College of Education, where she teaches courses in the foundations area and curriculum and supervises teachers. As a curriculum specialist, she has contributed to the development of nonsexist and multicultural programs and materials. Her publications and research reflect her interests in issues of equity, the history of early childhood curriculum, young children's dramatic play and block building, and children's learning through play.